ORDINARY LIVES

edited by

CLIVE MURPHY

1 The Good Deeds of a Good Woman
by BEATRICE ALI
The memoirs of a street character

2 Born to Sing
by ALEXANDER HARTOG
The memoirs of an East End mantle presser

3 Four Acres and a Donkey
by S. A. B. ROGERS
The memoirs of a lavatory attendant

4 Love, Dears!
by MARJORIE GRAHAM
The memoirs of a former chorus girl

5 A Funny Old Quist
by EVAN ROGERS
The memoirs of a gamekeeper

6 Oiky
by LEN MILLS
The memoirs of a pigman

This, the sixth of my 'Ordinary Lives', concerns a humble family in rural Suffolk. Len Mills, who dictated the main sequence, was once an Unbeliever and a man of violence. He is now a man of gentleness and simple Faith, and he was introduced to me by Mrs Noëlle Leven of Bridge Street when we passed his cottage, in nearby Alpheton, during a Christmas walk.

I have seldom attempted to represent Mr Mills' accent on the printed page, and, time and time again, I have excluded 'and that', 'you know', 'you see'. A smile must be imagined, too,—the uncanny smile of someone who is certain that Divine Vengeance will be wreaked upon a world where even hideous cruelties to cats and to little children are perpetrated still.

For permission to add a hitherto unpublished part-history of Alpheton, I thank Mr Mills' father-in-law, Mr Eddie Mitchell. I also thank Mr Mills' wife, Cynthia, for permission to repeat a Message and a prayer.

Editor

OIKY

Len Mills

Oiky

Recorded 31st July to 26th August, 1977

DURHAM : DENNIS DOBSON

First published in Great Britain 1984 by
Dobson Books Ltd. Brancepeth Castle, Durham

Photoset in Great Britain by
Photobooks (Bristol) Ltd.

ISBN 0 234 72257 6

I dedicate this book
to
my beloved wife,
Cynthia

Chapter One

Last Thursday morning [28th July, 1977] I went to the West Suffolk Hospital, Bury St Edmunds, for my check-up for that dreaded disease of cancer. I can praise the Lord for His mighty power and His wonderful power of healing. Three years ago this August I knew I had that disease. There is no trace, no sign whatever of cancer now. Dr Bratherton, the cancer specialist, felt me all over—felt under my arms, pressed all my body about, thumped my back. 'Mr Mills,' he say, 'you've nothing to worry about now. Come and see us in a year's time and we'll see how things are then. I don't know,' he say, 'I can't understand it. We expected more trouble from you because it was so bad. Though the lump weren't very big outwardly,' he said, 'do you know, Mr Mills,' he said, 'inside you it was the size of a football?' So I say, 'I didn't know, doctor.' He said, 'Well it was! We didn't know that the radium treatment would help to cure you. You've a lot to be thankful for.' I said, 'It's through my wife and it's thanks to the doctors and thanks to God that I'm still alive to tell the tale.'

Anyone who may read this and is suffering from cancer, I would like to tell them to put their trust in God because God can work wonderful miracles. I know that many people today say there's no such things as miracles, there's no such thing as healing. But I have seen the mighty works of God's hands in these past three years. I know I have no College training, I've had no education, I've never been to Bible College. I know I'm only just a farmworker, a clodhopper as they say in Suffolk. But God has helped me and I know that He will help others who will trust in Him. I would like others to know, I would like them never to say that there is no God, because I know and believe from the bottom of my heart that there is a God worth knowing and worth having as our Saviour. He is my Saviour because He healed me with a touch of His loving hand. I have had some wonderful experiences these last three years. I did not know before, though I went to church Sunday by Sunday, I did not know of His real love and His real power until I had cancer. Whoever may read this of my life and healing, please will they trust God for His love and for that healing power. Because God *does* heal. We know it—me, my wife Cynthia and my daughter Judith. At the time I was in hospital Judith cried and cried and said, 'Won't we ever have Daddy back, Mummy? Daddy *is* coming back, isn't he, Mummy? I don't want to lose Daddy, Mummy!' And I did come back. He brought me through from sickness into health, made perfectly whole in His name and in His love.

Three years ago I noticed this lump on my side yet I wasn't bothered, I wasn't caring at all. My wife, she forced me and begged of me to go to the doctor's, and the dear old doctor—she's retired now, Dr Margaret Hamp—she had an idea of what it was because she'd had it herself, and she asked the doctor what it is now for a second opinion, Dr Tom Penistan. I didn't know, my wife didn't know that the cancer roots were starting to work their way round to my spine, starting to travel up my back towards my brain. If I had left it another month it would have been too late.

My employer's wife, Mrs Rix, she took me in to Bury Hospital in the Humber on Thursday the 22nd of August. Got there at ten o'clock. There was about eight of us in the ward. Had lunch beside the bed—potatoes, peas and gravy.

In the afternoon I watched television in the special room and then a house surgeon in a white overall cleaned me up and shaved me. For supper I had leek soup and salad and a cup of tea. From midnight onward I was allowed nothing in my mouth. I slept well. Got up the next day at half past five, had a bath, weren't allowed no tea or drink or nothing, and, quarter to ten, a nurse came round and said, 'I'm just going to give you a pre-med.' and she gave that to me in my leg to calm me down. Ten o'clock they put me on one of those beds what you can raise up and down and wheel. They wheeled me down to the anaesthetic room and, outside, they lifted me off the bed and put me onto another one, put the sides up so I couldn't fall off, and wheeled me in. The anaesthetist said, 'Let's have a look at your lump.' He looked at it and then he gave me an injection in a vein in the back of my right hand. I never saw the operating theatre—I woke up in bed in the afternoon after Dr Williams done the operation. One of the nurses said, 'Hello, Mr Mills! Would you like a drink?' and she gave me a little sip of water.

At six o'clock they came round with supper. I was really surprised that I was allowed anything to eat. They said, 'You can have anything light' so I had some leek soup again and some salad—you know, lettuce, tomato and that—and a cup of tea.

The next day, Saturday, everything went fine. At half past five when they come round to wake you up and give you a cup of tea and let you have your wash and everything else, a Chinese nurse, Lee Chang was her name, she said, 'You can get out of bed today, Mr Mills.' I said, 'I can?!!' She said, 'Yes.' I was a bit unsteady at first like, you know, but I went to the bathroom and had my wash. I was in terrible agony because the stitches were sort of pulling. For breakfast I had porridge, egg, bread and butter and marmalade and a cup of tea. That was about eight. After breakfast I sat by the window looking at the out-patients coming and going. There weren't nothing much to do like, except sit and read the Daily Mirror and listen to Radio One on the bed with my earphones on. They come round at ten o'clock with a cup of tea or whatever you wanted—Oxo, Bovril. I'd a cup of Bovril. Lunch you have a menu come round, a card with various items on, and you could choose what you liked. I had cream potatoes, roast lamb and cauliflower and trifle. Sat by the window all afternoon and walked up and down the length of the corridor, slowly like, sort of crawling along. In the evening Mr Kirby came in with my wife and Judith, and had a word of prayer. He's one of the Free Church preachers that comes to the Mission Room in Bridge Street from time to time. He works for CAV as an engineer. I was having a hearty supper—fish and chips, and Arctic Roll to finish. He thanked God for His goodness and for bringing me through the operation. I said I'd been sitting at the side of the bed and walking and everything. He said, 'I shall have to increase my faith if you can do all that after an operation!' On the Friday night, after the operation, the doctors kept coming. 'Sorry to wake you up but we have to do it.' But on the Saturday I didn't see any doctors at all.

On the Sunday they phoned the wife up at two o'clock through Mr Rix and told her that I could come home. A preacher called Mr Chapman was coming to see me from Sudbury. Mr Rix phoned him up and said he'd come and get me but Mr Chapman said, 'I promised I'd go and see him', so he came and brought me home. I arrived back at about three o'clock. Poor old boy, he'd to go into the same hospital himself four days after, and he's just a cabbage now. His mind's gone and everything, and he was such a wonderful preacher. The wife and Judith were going to go to chapel that afternoon with a packed tea and then come to the hospital afterwards. So only Judith went, and she came with Mr Chapman in the car and helped me home to Alpheton from the hospital and stayed with me within the house and made a right fuss of me. I had three months off work, going up the farm just for odd days. Mr Rix gave me my wages which was a great help, and when the insurance money came through I paid that amount back. My wages then was about £26 net and the sickness benefit was about £18 so he paid me about £8.

On Tuesday the 27th a nurse came in from Acton just this side of Sudbury and took the stitches out. Then I went into hospital the day after for the Path Report but it wasn't through. The following Wednesday the report was through and it was a bad one. What was cut away had been sent to Addenbrooke's Hospital in Cambridge for analysis under microscopes and that, and Dr Bratherton at Bury St Edmunds he told me, 'I want you to come in to Cambridge for Radium treatment for a month.' When I told the wife, she was worried out of her wits. She was so upset she didn't realise what she was saying, she just let it go. She kept saying, 'That's the finish of you! . . . That's the finish of you!' My father's father died with cancer in the throat, and she lost her grandmother with it in the womb, and her grandfather had it on the back of his head—there was a plane crash during the war, he heard the bang and he went out to see where the blaze was, a motorbike just caught his coat and knocked him down and a bit of dirt got in his ear and he got cancer and it ate his ear right off.

I went to Cambridge in the hospital Volvo on September 16th, 17th, 18th, 19th, 20th, 23rd, 24th, 25th, 26th, 27th, 30th and October 1st, 2nd, 3rd, 4th, 7th, 8th, 9th, 10th and 11th. Dr Sewoski or something, a Polish chap, was the first person to see me. 'Hello! We're going to mark you out,' he said. There was what I should say would be a sort of camera and nurses and students were all round and they marked off a sort of square on my stomach and my back the same and they took photographs and they said, 'We want you in this position . . . and now we want you in this position.' Then they said,

'We'll take you further along to see somebody else now' and there they just gave me one quick zzz of radium treatment just to get me into the way of it like, you know. I lay on a bed and a big thing with lead blocks came down on me and a light shone down through a gap in the top on the square they wanted. The radiologist was Mrs Bratherton, the wife of Dr Bratherton, the cancer specialist. The radiologist and all the nurses and that don't stay in the room with you. They go out in case they get affected with this radium stuff and they've got a big thing on which they set all different dials and switches, and all at once this machine starts up and goes zzz and they see you the whole time on closed circuit television. I was given a prescription for some tablets to ward off sleepiness and then I had a cup of coffee in the canteen run by the WVS and went home.

I'd had my treatment for about a fortnight, then I had to go and meet Dr Bratherton to see how things were going. He pressed me around and said, 'I hope we ain't making you too sleepy.' I said, 'No, I'm not too sleepy at the moment but it makes me feel rotten.' He said. 'Yes, I know, but it's for your own good.'

When you arrive you go straight in the hospital entrance, stick your card in at the Reception Desk, sit down and the nurse and that see you sitting there and when you're ready to be called they just say, 'Mr Mills!' and you go in, off your jacket, down your trousers and lie on the bed. Nearly every day you have these students coming in. One day a group came in with Dr Fairlie the leukaemia specialist that was killed in 1975 by the I.R.A. In the end they were bringing the machine down closer and closer and letting it go zzzzzzz for three minutes.

There were as many as thirty going to Addenbrooke's for the same treatment. There were two old dear souls and the three of us got talking together of God's love and of His healing. There were others sitting around us and we were talking and praising God for all His wondrous works and His wondrous grace and His wondrous love towards us, and they didn't walk away—they sat and listened with attentive ear. Some were suffering more than I was. Some had it in the throat. Some had lung cancer. Yet they were trusting God for a miracle to happen.

At home, the wife's faith had wavered from the Lord. She was keeping right on about how I was finished. She was working at the Alpheton Garage—it's a cafe and service station combined—and saying 'Len won't be no more good!' I had to tell her off about it. She upset me. She made me cry. I used to grab hold of her and give her a good shove. One night I picked up three or four dinner plates and I just dropped them down in the sink. Another time I got so depressed I was going to go down the farm and get the twelve bore and blow myself to pieces. I kept saying there was no God, there was no God, why did He allow this thing to happen to me, one who loved and one who trusted Him. The wife had to call in Dr Hamp who gave me a fair talking to like and told me to pull myself together.

On the last Tuesday of my treatment, Tuesday the 8th of October, 1974, I came home from work and my wife she didn't know what to do—I was sick here there and everywhere. She said to me, 'It doesn't look as if *you'll* be going out tomorrow to Sudbury!'—on the Wednesday night we were going to the Great Crusade of Divine Healing and Spiritual Inspiration at All Saints, the Church of England church in Sudbury. I said, 'Don't talk so silly, don't! I shall be all right!' And when I came home on the Wednesday night I believed that God was working a miracle out then because I found Cynthia at the door all smiles and happy. She said, 'Do you feel like going tonight?' I said, 'Yes. Mr Kirby's coming for us and I'm going.' Mr Kirby met us at the door. He said to me, 'You look happy tonight then!' The wife said, 'Yes. Different to what he was yesterday! He was vomiting all over the place, couldn't keep *nothing* down!'

When we got to the meeting, they had hymns, choruses, prayers, clapping hands, rejoicing and praising God—it was a real joyful meeting. At first, the Rev. Trevor Dearing, he called out those who wanted to be saved and give their lives to Jesus Christ. And after that part of the meeting was gone, he called out for those who needed healing, a touch of the hands. There was people going forward for nervous depression, rheumatics, people deaf, blind, in wheel chairs. Then he gave out for those who were suffering from cancer. I went up to the front. It wasn't the Rev. Trevor Dearing who laid hands on me—it was his assistant, the Rev. Warboys. He laid his hands on my head and, as he was praying for me, I went flat out, flat out on the floor, and lay there almost senseless for five minutes. I could feel a burning and a tingling sensation in my side. And all at once it stopped. I came to, got up and walked back to my place, to my dear wife and dear daughter who were crying, there were tears of joy streaming down their faces to see that that miracle had happened. And the very next week I had to go to Bury for a check-up and I saw Dr Bratherton. He said, 'Well, Mr Mills,' he said, 'you've done a wonderful job of work on your side. There's no sign of what happened to you!' I said, 'God has worked a miracle on me!' He said, 'Thank God for the miracle then,' he said, 'because we expected you to have to come back to Cambridge again for more treatment. And even with the treatment we didn't think that we'd be able to do any good with you. We thought that you were going to die. We didn't expect you to live the rest of the year through. Thank God for that miracle upon your body and come and see us again in a month's time.' I said, 'All right, doctor.' And in a month's time everything was still fine. Dr Bratherton said, 'Come and see us in three months' time.' I went in three months' time and everything was still all right then. I had about three sessions of three months, then he said, 'Come and see us in six months.' And everything was still all right then. And another six months' time was up this Thursday.

A month after God worked that miracle upon me I went down to another Trevor Dearing meeting, and the parish rector who was there, the Rev. Blackall, asked me to give a word of testimony. I said, 'All right, then' and during the meeting I was asked to take over and speak of my healing. Everything was put on tape so people could buy a tape of the whole service. The tape-recorder was like a big studio one you'd see at the B.B.C. in London with different knobs on. I got up in front of the microphone and I told the congregation there how I had cancer, had this radium treatment and came down to All Saints on that Wednesday night and came out for healing power. And I told them with assurance that God had healed me that night. There was a great hush in the congregation. They listened with attentive ear as I spoke to them of my healing and I spoke of my unbelief, how I had said there was no God, why should He allow this to happen to me, one who loved Him. But now, I said, I can rejoice with joy that I know there is a God, because He has healed me and I am able to do the work I love to do, work on the land, once again to lift the bags of meal and bales of straw, which I couldn't do before, and handle the pigs and that with no ill-feeling at all. And I said I went to the doctor and the doctor said, 'It's a miracle!' And the Rev. Trevor Dearing hollered out, 'Praise God! It's wonderful when doctors can say there's been a miracle!'

Before I was healed I didn't love the Lord so much as I do now. Since He healed me I've loved Him ten times more, I feel that I've been led to do healing work through Him healing me. My dear mother-in-law, father-in-law, wife and daughter were down on their bended knees praying that God would work out a miracle for me. And that miracle happened at All Saints Church in Sudbury. A servant of God was there, the Rev. Trevor Dearing, and God worked that miracle upon me. God has looked after us, He has kept us and kept us safe through these past three years. Yes, we have a lot to thank our Lord for. He is with us day by day. We can see the wonderful works of His hands as we go about this world of His—His love, His care for us, our family here. He drew me to the source of His love and His tender care at that time of most serious illness when I was at death's door. I know that God wants me to speak of Him, to go about His work and to tell others of my healing and of His saving grace.

Chapter Two

The following prayers and message were spoken by Mr Mills during evening worship at the Free Church Mission Room, Bridge Street, Suffolk, on Sunday, 7th August, 1977:—

Shall we ask the Lord's blessing upon our gathering together tonight? O God, our loving heavenly Father, we gather here once again before You in the attitude of prayer. We thank Thee, Lord, for the fellowship we had this afternoon, and, Lord, we pray that You will come amongst us again this evening now. Lord, we thank Thee for what Thou has done for us. And, Lord, may we come with ever joyful hearts praising and thanking Thee for all the care bestowed upon us. We thank Thee, Lord, for Thy healing hand laid upon Charlie. It is a joy too see him here amongst us once again. And we pray, Lord, that Thy hand shall still be upon him and that he will make a speedy and full recovery to health and strength once again. I know, Lord, that You are able to heal all our diseases if we come in faith. Increase our faith, Lord, because, Lord, we know today that there are false Christs among us who say that they are the Lord and are not. Lord, we pray that You will give us the courage to stand against the wiles of the Devil, that we will come to Thee and You will put Your hand in ours and guide us along the road of life. We pray for other gatherings up and down this land, and behind the Iron Curtain where they dare not gather as we are, they have to gather underground or in a secret place for fear of the secret police. Yet, Lord, they are crying out for Your word over there. Lord, many people risk their lives over there or are being cast into prison for life sentences for taking bibles into that land. We pray, Lord, that You will go with them and keep them safe so that Thy word will be glorified. Lord, we know in this land of ours that we are not so ready and willing to do what they do out there. We pray, Lord, that You will wake us up out of our sleep because the time, O Lord, is drawing nigh, very fast, we believe, when Thou shalt return to this earth to take us who are blind to be redeemed for evermore. Lord, we know that many relations of ours and others around this land do know Thee not. Lord, it would grieve our hearts to let them go down to a lost eternity, to the everlasting lake of fire. Yes, Lord, there is going to be an everlasting lake of fire. Thy word proclaims it. Lord, like Abraham of old, when he was amongst that fire, he was so thirsty that he wanted to dip his finger in water to ease his parched throat, yet, Lord, it was no good because he did not do what You wanted him to—Lord, we pray that You will be with us and that Thy word shall go forth in this place tonight that others may hear that still, small voice and come in and sup with Thee. Be with us Lord, as we continue here with Thee. And now we will say the prayer that Jesus taught His disciples to say when He was here upon earth: Our Father . . .

Let us pray. Our loving Heavenly Father, we pray, Lord, that You will accept these gifts given to Thee by Thy children. Lord, You first gave Your life for us, and, Lord, we are willing to give our lives to Thee because, Lord, if we lay down our lives for Thee, Thou wilt take them up again. Everyone won't be ready to be made alive on the Last Day. Help us, Lord, to go forth in these last days out into the by ways and the hedges to compel them to come in because Lord, like it was just said, life is very brief. Yes, Lord, we know not when the time comes for us to die. Like my father, Lord, who went out to an Agricultural Show at Hadleigh, came home and died in bed during the night—no time, Lord, was there to bring him to Thee. He made a mockery of Your truth and Your cross. He threatened, Lord, to burn the Holy Bible. Yes, Lord, he is gone down to a lost eternity. We pray, Lord, for the rest of my family that they will come to Thee so that we can be one happy family in Christ Jesus. We know, Lord, that my sister [Mr Mills' step-sister, May] went into hospital for a serious operation and she did not give Thee the thanks that was due to Thee for bringing her through. Yes, our faith brings us through. You brought me through, a strong and healthy man once again. Yes, Lord, Your touch still has its ancient power, and we pray, Lord, that many would believe that today. This we ask in Your name. Amen.

If anybody wants a text for today, they should read the Second Epistle to Peter, Chapter Three, verse three: 'Knowing this first, that there shall come in the last days scoffers, walking after their own lusts . . .'. Yes, it's true, my friends, that we *are* living in the last days. It was only a few days ago in the newspaper that there was a man who believed that he was sent down from heaven, that he was sent back down from heaven by God. He was proclaiming to be the Christ. The whole centre page was full of it—that he had wonderful healing power in his hands, he could heal all aches and pains, that he believed that he was sent down by God from heaven. I don't believe that at all. There was only one man sent down from heaven as a baby, and that was Our Lord and Saviour, Jesus Christ. He was the only one who came down. You can see, my friends, that we have false Christs, false witnesses and false servants today. They come to your doors with false things. It's like you see in adverts.—this soap-powder washes whiter, and *this* soap-powder washes whiter, whiter than snow. There only is one thing that will wash us whiter, and that is the blood of Jesus Christ, our Saviour. And yet men will come to your door and say, 'I am the Christ. I can help you. I can do anything for you.' Just turn them away because it's not true! All you have to do is ask them, 'Let me see the nail-prints in your hands and let me see that sword-riven side!' as doubting Thomas did. *He* wouldn't believe until he saw that sword-riven side and those nail-pierced hands! He wanted to see first before he believed. Yes, people may come to your door but they must have the nail-pierced hands and that sword-riven side before they can tell you that they are the Christ. There are many false prophets today. It's like that hymn what my wife sang a few minutes ago. We've got to be in time. We've got to stay awake and waiting for the true Messiah when He comes. Yes, because it's not going to be long before He'll come. So, my friends, we have false prophets in our Church and in our Mission Halls today. They proclaim false messages. I know of one church where you dare not preach about Jesus Christ—they say they want a joyful message, not a morbid one. But this one *is* a joyful message—the blood of Jesus Christ—for where would we be today if Jesus had not shed His blood there upon that cross? We wouldn't be found here today rejoicing and giving Him praise and all the joy for what He has done for us! He's a wonderful saviour and the only one! Yes, you see many false prophets coming today, false messengers; false words they proclaim. Yes, false words. It says at the end of The Book of Revelations, Chapter Twenty-two, that any man taketh away a word from this book or add others to it he shall lose his place in the Eternal Glory. Yet it's happening today that false words are being added and others taken away. You read the new versions of the Bible! All untrue. This bible here (the Authorised Version) is the only true one. I know we have got many versions of bibles in our house but, there, more often than not, we use the Good Old Book because every word in there is true. Yes, false prophets. Yes, we've got to be in time because life at best is very brief. If we went about proclaiming false messages, false words to those that believe in Christ . . . Yes, we've got to look at ourselves as well. We must not proclaim false words. We must proclaim the truth, the truth of Jesus and His love and of His salvation. Yes, many have left the churches today, many have turned their back upon God. They want nothing to do with Him. They would rather have the pleasures of this world today. Yes, I knew what the pleasures of the world were like until I found my Saviour! Yes, I knew when I couldn't walk the white line straight through drink! Yes, all my money was spent on drink. Night after night I went to the public house, drinking my soul away until Jesus found me. You get people today, I'm not throwing stones but you get people who say, 'I can't give it up, I can't do this and I can't do that.' Let me tell you you can. They've only to look to that One above. He is always willing and ready to help. He helped *me* in my time of need. 'Yes,' I said to myself, I said, 'if this is the wiles of drink, I've finished with it.' And I never entered a public house for drink anymore. You see, you must have a strong faith in God to do that. Oh yes, *I* haven't been all I should be. No, I haven't. No, I weren't all I should be to my beloved wife. I used to be cruel to her in many ways. Yet she stood by me in thick and thin, she never left me. She always stood by me, horrible as I was to her until I came into repentance and truth to the Lord Jesus Christ at Bury St Edmunds, a meeting there conducted by the Reverend Bill Bathman. Yes, it looked that night as if he was pointing a finger at me and saying all the horrible things that I said to my wife—yes, I even knocked her about—, and it looked that night as if that servant of God was pointing a finger at me because all the words he said were true. And there that night I came in truth and full repentance to God. And I never looked back on that night because now we are happy together, serving the one and only true God. Yes, our home is happy. We have a daughter who loves the Lord Jesus Christ, as well.

Anyone is welcome to our home. The door is ever open for friends and loved ones to come in. Yes, there would be a time when no one would come in because of my drinking and suchlike. Yes, we truly love that God now. You see we don't go about scoffing about this, that and the other because we have this and we have that. Our home is humble. More often than not we haven't two halfpennies to rub together. Yet we are happy because the Lord always provides our needs. We have never been without food. We never have been without drink—tea and suchlike I'm talking about. Yes, if at home you go down on your bended knee, God is always willing and ready to help. Yes, I know I kept this from my wife because I did not want to worry her at the time. When I had that cancer I went to Cambridge for the treatment and the doctors told me there and then, 'We don't know whether we shall be able to cure you. There may be no hope.' Yet God saw me through. He saw me through that time of trouble and worry. And—praise His holy name—He healed me. That was three years ago, and only the other week I went to Bury after six months had lapsed, the six months' date was up on the 28th of July. I went into the doctor's consulting room, he examined me from head to toe, he say, 'Mr Mills, there's no trace of nothing. Everything is complete. We don't want to see you no more for a year.' So you see, my friends, God is a true God. Those who proclaim that they are the Christ would never be able to do that. They would never be able to heal your sick body unless they were one of Christ, who would be able to heal you through their hands. Man cannot heal you. It is God himself, working through His servants. I am longing for the day—and I believe that the Lord is calling me into His healing ministry—yes, I'm longing for that day to come to pass when we shall be able to have healing meetings and praise meetings here, bring the sick in to give them the laying on of hands and bring them back to health and strength. Yes, I know the Lord sometimes will hear the answer, that by right we of Christ have the right to be healed. We have the right to come to His table and to sup with Him and we have the right to be with Him in glory, we have the right to sit with Him in heaven. I wonder when it will be that He calls us home and we have to face Him face to face, when we have brought Him wheat, barley or tares or hay or chaff, and He will say to us, 'Well done, thou good and faithful servant.' But what would it be if we would have to bow our heads and hang our heads before Him in shame and in sorrow for what we have not done? Yes, we must work for Him. We must go and tell these scoffers who are walking after their own lusts that there is a true and living Christ who died for them as well as us, and He is willing, ready and waiting to come to them and to take them in His arms and bless them. Yes, let us be in time, because life at best is very brief. We're in time here, I trust. When Jesus shall come to take us we shall be with Him for evermore. Amen.

Let us pray. O God, our Loving Heavenly Father, I know, Lord, that You will go with us. Keep us safe from the dangers of this world, and keep us safe from evil scoffers and evil Christs, Lord, who proclaim to be You and are not. Let us go out now in peace to the world and proclaim the true and living Christ to others that they may come in here and fill these chairs before it is too late. It's true: life at best is very brief. Lord, we trust here tonight that every one of us shall be in time to meet Thee in the air when Thou shalt come to take us to be with Thee for evermore. O Lord, we have a lot to thank Thee for, for dying for us miserable sinners here on earth. Yes, You died in our place that we might live. And we trust that others tonight, Lord, may come and live. Yes, Lord, there is life for a look at You. May they come, Lord, and see those nail-pierced hands and that sword-riven side which flowed that life-giving flow. Soon, we believe, that that life-giving flow will cease when this wicked earth shall be destroyed by everlasting fire. O Lord, what of those that shall be left behind? Yes, an everlasting torment for those who believe not. O Father, let us proclaim the Gospel message. The story must be told. Help us, Lord, to tell it to others. This we ask in that name of Thine. Amen.

Chapter Three

I didn't believe in God as a boy. I didn't believe in Him till I was twenty-five. There was a pal of mine who worked with me as a cowman at Newton and he asked me one Sunday afternoon would I go to the chapel with him because he was an out-and-out believer. His name was John. He said, 'Will you come with me to the chapel this afternoon at Newton?' I said, 'No, I'm going to a motorbike scramble.' And off I went full of joy with my pals to the scramble at Cockfield and I nearly got there, then I had an accident—I went over the top of the handlebars of my pushbike going down a hill. So I thought to myself, 'This wouldn't have happened if I was going to the chapel with John.' I considered a lot that afternoon about Jesus. I thought that He made this accident to happen to me because I refused to go to chapel, and from that great day on I never went to another scramble, I was always found in Newton Methodist Chapel.

Not long after,—in 1957, September or October—I met my wife. Her name was Cynthia Mitchell then. She was a nice-looking girl with black hair and glasses. A nice, kindly, friendly girl she was. And she came over to Newton Methodist Chapel with her father to a mid-week meeting, Wednesday, seven thirty, to show these lantern slides of *The Pilgrim's Progress* to raise funds for the Free Church. She was helping her father to put the slides into the lantern and she accidentally dropped one on the floor and I picked it up for her and then we got talking together and the following Wednesday I came over to the Free Church Mission Hall at Bridge Street for curiosity because they had a prayer meeting there every Wednesday night at half past six. (That's only stopped about three years ago.) Her father and mother and a farmworker called Charlie Cook and one or two dear old ladies were there. We had the prayer meeting, and Mr Mitchell asked me if I'd go up to their home in Buxton's Cottage, Alpheton, and have some supper. Buxton's Cottage is on Mr Rix's farm—Clapstile—where he was stockman till 1965. I said, 'No, I can't stop this time', so he said, 'Will you come over the Mission Hall next Sunday?' I said, 'Yes, O.K. I'll come over Sunday', and Cynthia was there and after the Gospel Service I went up to Buxton's Cottage, had supper with them and that's how Cynthia and me started going together.

The following Thursday was my day off, and we arranged to meet each other in Sudbury. She only did a little housework in the mornings at Alpheton Rectory and she always used to cycle in to Sudbury on a Thursday to do the shopping. We met on The Market Hill, done the shopping and I came over to her house for tea. We started going together regular then. We were going together nearly three years and then we married in 1960. Just under a year before, I asked her father if we could get engaged and that, and he said, 'Yes, Go ahead!' and I bought her a ring in a jeweller's shop in Bury St Edmunds, a silver ring with three imitation diamond stones in. I believe it cost me twenty pound. We had an engagement party in her house and I gave the ring during the party. Her mother and her father were there and my step-mother came over and we had ham sandwiches and tea.

We got married in St John's Methodist Church, Sudbury, on Saturday March the 26th at the start of the spring drilling. I'd got a job as a cowman with Dr Norman at Brundon Hall,

Sudbury, a month before. A tied cottage went with the job so we'd a proper home to go to. Three cottages were all joined together and we were in one of the end ones, No. 3.

The wedding was lovely. The minister was the Rev. Richard Hailwood. I had to be there first with the best man, Cynthia's Uncle Sam. Cynthia came later with her father. I was wearing a grey suit and a white carnation. She was wearing all white with a veil and a bouquet of red tulips and narcissi and lucky horseshoes. I gave her a bible and I gave the two bridesmaids, her first cousins, New Testaments. The best man was more nervous than what I was. He was shaking like a leaf. I say, 'Are you nervous?' He say, 'I'm scared stiff!' We sat there waiting and then, at 2.30, the organ struck up *Here Comes The Bride* and then I got up and stood at the altar waiting to meet my bride. He had the ring—gold. It cost me about £8. I didn't get a ring from her—you can do if you want to but.

The church was absolutely full, it was *packed.* A lot of them was from the different churches where Cynthia used to preach. The minister said to us afterwards, 'If I can't fill the church, Cynthia,' he say, 'you can!' They put in the *East Anglian Daily Times* LOCAL PREACHER MARRIES. We had the hymns *Love Divine, All Loves Excelling* and *The Lord Is My Shepherd* and the marriage vows and all that, and the minister gave a little address and said how we both loved Jesus. Then we had Holy Communion.

The Rev. Hailwood was a very jovial fellow; he used to make you roar laughing. He showed a film once at the Mission Room and afterwards he say, 'Have you got time for a quick one?' as we passed The Rose and Crown! He was very tiny and he had a deformed back with his head in one shoulder. He died the following January, ten months after we were married. His wife told us he said he would die within seven years of coming to St John's and he did. If he hadn't have had a deformed back they could have got him into an iron lung—or was it an oxygen tent?—and saved his life. He worked Cynthia very hard. She'd a circuit of nine churches. Some Sundays she had three appointments. One Sunday she was at Glemsford in the morning, preaching and taking the service, then the same thing in the afternoon at Leavenheath, and the same again in the evening at Long Melford. She went on like that till Judith was born because when Hailwood died she worked just as hard for the Rev. Malcolm Carter who followed him. Then one day he told her she wouldn't be on the preachers' future plan.

After the marriage service we went back in the car alone to Alpheton and stood at the door of the Village Hall to welcome the guests in to the reception. We'd asked the minister could we have the reception in the Church Hall of St John's to stop running backwards and forwards between Sudbury and Alpheton and he said, 'Will there be any drink?' We say, 'Just the port and that to toast the bride and groom' and he said, 'No, sorry. I can't have it.' (The Methodists was against drink till about three years ago when they had a meeting and altered the laws.) But he come with his wife to the reception and toasted us in lemonade.

The presents were all on view. We got no end of different things—towels, blankets, Apostle spoons. The Minister and his wife gave a tablecloth and traycloth, both in blue and hand-embroidered by the wife with different coloured daisies. An electric iron that came from the Sunday School at Bridge Street, that's seventeen years old and hasn't had to have a new element or nothing in yet! And the electric kettle from the Mission Room congregation, that's the same! My father-in-law bought us a canteen of cutlery and my father bought us blankets. We've got things packed away somewhere and we've never even used them! We've still got the wedding dress. If Judith marries, we'll pass it on to her.

We had port and cider and tea and coffee, ham salads and trifles, quite a mixture of foods. My mother-in-law and father-in-law, they done it all theirselves. Mrs Eady, a housewife, and her daughter, Pam Green, helped them serve. It cost £70. I'd to pay Mr Howard at Long Melford for the cars. He only charged £5 for three cars on the go, Alpheton to Sudbury, Sudbury to Alpheton, Alpheton to Sudbury four or five times, and the Monday night he brought the wedding presents down for us to our home at Brundon. About seventy was at the reception. We asked Dr Norman would he like to come along but he was just getting over a heart attack so he couldn't—he couldn't take the excitement. We had a two-tier cake made by somebody in the village, and after we cut it everybody called out 'Speech!', 'Speech!' I thanked everybody very much for the lovely presents we'd had and for all for what everybody'd done and I promised I'd look after Cynthia well and treat her well. There were toasts to the bride and bridegroom: 'May they have many years' happiness together!' He kept making us two die laughing, the best man did, because he was a bit of a character, like. He say, 'You know where you want to put that tonight, don't you, Len?' and he pointed to a big round vase. 'You want to stick that under your bed!' He kept tormenting us like that and making us roar with laughing.

The reception lasted from four till nine. Then we left in the car for Cynthia's home and she changed out of her wedding dress and that, and then we ordered the car back again and we went to Brundon with the dress and that in a suitcase and with my Aunt Elsie—she must be getting on for ninety now. We opened the door, and there was an envelope lying on the floor with a five pound note in from my employer, Dr Norman. He also gave us an electric copper. Dr Norman was a wonderful employer. Time and time he'd give us things.

We sat talking and drinking tea. I was too shy to go to bed! We had three different lots of tea, then at one o'clock my wife she say, 'I'm going to bed!' she say. So we all went up together. Aunt Elsie went to her room and we went to our own and nature took its course. But we took precautions. We had no children for three years—till 1963. We planned it. I knew all about what to do from school experiences; we all used French letters at Nayland School. When we decided to have a child it happened first time, and our daughter, Judith, was born.

After we was married I was working most Sundays so I couldn't usually go to the afternoon services at the Mission Hall, Bridge Street, but when I had time to go at night I used to help Cynthia by singing solos accompanied by the organ or reciting poems such as, you know, 'The Little Donkey':

> Once on the hills of Palestine
> Outside the dusty town
> A little donkey with grey ears
> Romped gaily up and down . . .

She made my faith stronger but I was a very bad husband, very jealous. I used to be really cruel to her, knock her about. If I saw her talking to other men I'd go straight up in the bows, as they say, fly right off the handle like. I were jealous when she joined The Youth for Christ Choir for a special crusade at Bury in case she'd mess about with other men. I'd hit her on the face, anywhere. When she was carrying the daughter, I even punched her in the stomach and threw her across the kitchen. Dr Hamp called me a two-faced little bastard and a pig and said I'd caused so much trouble she'd have to have a Caesarian for the baby to be born. My father-in-law threatened to get the solicitors and separate us, it was *that* bad. Then, one evening, we went to a meeting at Bury St Edmunds conducted by the Rev. Bill Bathman. By chance he was talking about bad husbands and being in sin, and he pointed his finger and it seemed he was pointing it straight at me. It was a coincidence like, you know. He was saying, 'You won't have a second chance. You've got to be kind to others.

You musn't have jealousy in your heart; you've got to get that out of your heart if you're going to believe in Jesus; Jesus don't like jealousy.' I started to cry, and at the end of the service, you know, you have to go up to be counselled, you go to a counselling room, and Mr Mason from Whepstead—the dear old boy, he's passed on now—he counselled me and gave me a leaflet to read and I made a confession of faith and signed and prayed I would believe in the Lord Jesus Christ and be saved, and from then on everything got better and hardly ever did I hit my wife. Mr Mason used to come and see me at the house every so often to see how I was going on and he told his wife it was a genuine conversion and whenever he came over to our Bridge Street Mission Hall to preach he used to say to me, 'Ah, it was a lovely time that night at the Town Hall, weren't it, Len?!' He always used to come over and say that.

We've only had about two real bust-ups since. About two years ago, one Saturday afternoon, the front wheel had gone on my bicycle and I wanted just a wheel—I give her all my wages to keep—and she reckoned Fred Elliott of Alpheton wanted to change too much and I'd get it cheaper in Sudbury, and we argued and argued and I was getting hotter and hotter under the collar and I just sent my fist out right under her chin. She said, 'Go for the police, Judith!' so Judith runs round the neighbour's, Mrs Campbell, and Mrs Campbell phoned the police and the police came and wanted to know what was wrong. My wife told them and they say it was no police matter. She said, 'It ain't no police matter?!' and one of them say, 'No, we can't do nothing about it, my dear. It's a domestic affair and we can't interfere. There's only one thing you can do and it's to go to your solicitors and then you can either get a separation or a divorce.' If I was really violent and cut her up and that, you know, then they could have done something, but over a tiffle like that they couldn't do nothing. He say to me, 'I've only got one thing to say to you,' he say, and that's "Grow up!"' I blinking near hit him. Then I *would* have been for it, hitting a police officer! We made it up afterwards. I bought her sweets and chocolates and flowers in Sudbury. There's never been any violence since. That was the lot. Nothing any more.

The other bust-up we had was down at Brundon, at Norman's. About two years before we came up here to Clapstile Farm and Mr Rix, Cynthia took somebody in out of pity more than anything, but he weren't what he should have been, you know, he was just a rogue, and she thought more of him than she did of me, she was giving him more attention than what she was me. He came to the Mission Room one Sunday with a friend of ours who said he was Ron Flatman. He wore a dog collar and a cloak and he took the service the same night and said he was an ex-alcoholic, you know, and used to sleep round and that along the Thames Embankment, and before that he was a Baptist minister for four years with a church in London and was Chaplain to the Girls' Brigade and Chaplain to the Boys' Brigade. My wife more or less idolised him. He came down to us and asked for meals once or twice and he just sort of found his way in like, saying he weren't happy. He stayed at our house on and off for about a year. I got so as I thought Cynthia was carrying on with him. I used to get wild and hit her. She said they weren't having an affair at all, I'd no need to be jealous. But anybody would be, wouldn't they?, having to do the crocks while she sat next to him talking after a meal. I nearly did away with myself. I took phenobarbitone and was writhing in pain and Ron—he was supposed to have been a nurse in a hospital as well—he knew exactly what to do and got me some salt water and made me sick. In the end he went and rented a bedsitter from a woman in Sudbury. If he had stayed much longer two of Cynthia's cousins were coming down to throw him out. He and Cynthia had an argument with my father-in-law about it all and we left the Mission Room for nearly a year.

Then we began to find out different things. There was a

visiting speaker coming to a church in Sudbury. 'Yes,' he say to me, 'I know that man right well. You know what? Look here, my friend,' he say, 'he's a married man and he's run away from his wife and four children and he's never had no charge of a church at all.' And we used to have communion with him in our own home! We'd break the bread and drink the black currant, he'd go through the whole service! We faced it out with him that we'd heard he wasn't a minister and that he was married, and he went all quiet, never said a word.

He used to do odd jobs. All at once he came down to us on a Friday night about a fortnight before Christmas and said he was going to buy us a chicken and that and then he say, 'Len, will you come up to Sudbury with me tomorrow and help me point up a chimney? I daren't go up the ladder high because of my heart.' He say, 'I'll come down and pick you up in the car about one o'clock.' He said he'd pay me well, and I wanted the money, so I say, 'Right-o, Ron. I'll be waiting for you.' I kept waiting. Half past one, two o'clock, three o'clock—nobody turned up. We knew he was working for a joiner in Sudbury so I went to this chap,—I believe it was Mr Benson his name was—went to see him and spoke to him and say there's no Mr Flatman. He say, 'He come first thing this morning,' he say, 'and took thirty pound off of me in advance before doing some work and he's gone to Norwich to do his Christmas shopping.' I phoned up the Norwich Hospital in case he'd had a heart attack but nobody of that name had been brought in. I went up to his flat to see if he'd turned up and I see the landlady and she told me not to worry, he wouldn't be back till Wednesday.

Nobody saw him again. He left owing three weeks' rent and he took the flat keys and all! He'd left behind his clerical robes and his chalice and the plate thing you put the bread on. The landlady made us sign for some pillowcases we'd given him and some saucepans to say that they were ours so if the police come she were in the clear, and she told us, 'You'd better hand the rest over,' she say, 'because you must assume they're stolen property.' When we went up to the police with the chap who was employing him and wanted his thirty pound back, they said they couldn't do much yet because he was quite free to go off when he liked and where he wanted to but if he ever came back we could make a charge. But he never did turn up from that day to this. He'd accounts everywhere. He owed the Co-op money. He'd started off a Club with somebody else and owed him twelve pound. Six months after he disappeared they say to me at the Co-op, 'We won't worry about this account now, mate. He's been found dead in a derelict London house.' But the police have never said nothing to us or that so we don't know whether he's alive or dead. Mr Chapman said, 'He's too blinking crafty to die!'

He was a wolf in sheep's clothing. And he tried to part me and Cynthia, she'll admit it herself. He used to say, 'Marriages aren't made in heaven. You can go with who you like and when you like.' But I believe in marriage. We've never been unfaithful to one another. We've been together seventeen years and she's never had an affair with another man. I just had this fear in my mind that she was carrying on with Ron Flatman. And I've never had an affair with another woman. I talk to different women and that, you know, and sometimes I go down to Bridge Street and take a dozen eggs to a woman down there and her husband's out and that, but there's nothing in it.

If you want to have a happy marriage it's no good one pulling one way and one pulling the other, you've got to pull together as we have done in the past few years, especially when I was ill when we pulled together really well, we really loved each other. That's the way to go on. Broken marriages, these days there are so many of them! But I believe that trusting in the Lord will keep us together and keep anyone together who will put their trust in His hands. He is able to do all things as He has done for myself and my wife and daughter in the past years, and He will do the same for anyone who will only look to Him.

Several people say they can't imagine me losing my temper—someone once say to me it's as well I weren't a girl, I'd always be saying Yes! But I'm very quick. Just one word out of place and I'm straight up in the bows. I used to hit first and ask questions afterwards. I'm a lot calmer now. The wife used to say, 'You ain't done the chickens, you ain't cleaned the rabbits out yet!' I'd say, 'Give us a chance, dear.' She'd say, 'You've had plenty of time!'—then I'd start going up. But I never lose my temper on the farm, I always, you know, bring it home and let go then. My employers have told me from time to time, they say, 'If there's anything wrong on the farm tell *us* about it,' they say. 'Don't take it home to your wife.' I always used to get into trouble with Mr Paul Norman, Dr Norman's son, over that. Someone on the farm would tell me to do more work and this and that and the other and of course I'd bottle it up, you see, and let rip when I got home. I used to tell the wife what had gone wrong and she'd tell me, she'd say, 'It ain't no good bringing it home to me. Why not tell Mr Norman about it?' she say. I say, 'I daren't!' So *she* did, and Mr Norman came after me about it and said, 'Don't be afraid to tell me anything, Len. I shan't bite your head off.'

Judy was only three weeks away when Cynthia had that accident because we was arguing and I threw her across the kitchen. She was in labour a fortnight till the pains got so bad the doctor said, 'We'll have to get you off to hospital.' We took her off to Bury Hospital at eleven o'clock at night, or it was supposed to be eleven—the ambulance got lost, it went to Brandon instead of Brundon. They said, 'There'll be nothing to happen tonight.' Then about four o'clock time in the morning the police came to the door and told me to go to the hospital or phone the hospital so I phoned the hospital and they told me, 'Mr Mills,' says a nurse, 'you've got a daughter.' She say, 'We tried to contact you because we have to ask the husband's permission if we can operate. But you didn't want a dead baby on your hands, did you?' I say, 'No. Thank you very much. Can I come over?' She say, 'Yes. Your wife's round from the anaesthetic. You can come straight over. You can spend the day here if you like.' I told Dr Norman and he said, 'That's quite all right, Len. Off you go.' So I took a taxi around nine o'clock because there weren't no buses, and when I went in the wife lay there in a ward all on her own with tubes up her nose and having blood transfusions, and I was sat there with her and they told me when the bottle of glucose run out I'd got to ring the bell to help them so they wouldn't have to keep running in and out. When Cynthia see me arrive she had a good cry and put her arms round me. She say, 'We wanted to do it and we prayed for a daughter and we got a daughter. We knew that the Lord would give us what we wanted.' The nurse was a young Christian nurse. She said, 'Mrs Mills,' she said, 'your faith must have been very strong,' she said, 'to know even before the baby was born that you was going to have a daughter.' Yes, it's wonderful how these things happen. We wanted a girl before even the child was born. We reckon that girls are less trouble than what boys are. If it had been a boy, of course, we shouldn't have worried, we'd have loved it just as much as we do Judith. But we prayed for a girl and we knew that God would give us a girl. I wanted a girl, Cynthia wanted a girl, and the father-in-law wanted a girl as well. We all wanted a girl and, when that arrived, oh dear, full of joy everybody was that we'd got a girl! And we might have had another but Cynthia was thirty-five and, after the Caesarian operation, the doctors advised her not to as her age was against her. If she'd been in her twenties they'd have said, 'Go ahead and have another one!' It's too late now anyway. She'll be fifty next birthday and the cancer operation made me impotent—I can have sex but I can't produce children.

It was touch and go for the wife and the baby for three days, they were both on the danger list. Judy was in a room with a lot of other babies, all in different cots. A right pretty little girl she was, with dark hair. When she was a fortnight old we took her with us to the Mission Hall and she didn't cry at all. She was a very good baby—except before she was born. When the organ used to start up Cynthia used to say, 'Judith's a-kicking!'! Yes, Judy went to the Sunday School at Bridge Street when she was a fortnight old. My father-in-law ran it at half past two every Sunday till five years ago when he had a stroke and my wife took over. We had to close it about three months ago, the children just stopped coming. We went to see the parents about it and they say, 'They're nine or ten and they're old enough to do just as they like theirselves.' So Judith now comes to the afternoon service we have instead. She's never been away from church, only through illness, and that's the way I think children should be brought up.

And when a family come along you should take it in turns to look after it. When the baby woke at night I used to sometimes lift it up and give it its bottle and change it, you know. We used to have a laugh up the town. I used to take Judy on Saturdays sometimes in the pram and you'd meet another chap with a pram and he'd say, 'Hello, another learner!' The wives used to start cackling! But I don't believe that the man should do the shopping. I was in a shop up Sudbury once and a poor girl, she looked really scared of her husband. He was going round picking up the goods and putting them in the box. 'Do we want this?' and 'Do we want that?'—she daren't say Yes or No. I didn't think that should be. You should give the wife the housekeeping money and she should do the shopping. You can always help her in the house. Whenever Cynthia's queer, I cook. I make buns, jam tarts, mince pies. It seems strange for a man. I can make anything. When Cynthia and Judith go to Melford shopping on Saturdays I have all the dinner cooked for them when they come in. They'll have the Yorkshire pudding cooked, the meat cooked nice and brown, the potatoes, greens, peas, everything. I just do it all in my head, I've never read no cookery books or nothing. I'd sooner do cookery than I would gardening. My father-in-law can't cook and my own father he couldn't cook, but I think a man should be able to cook. If your wife is upstairs you're in a muddle otherwise. My wife's Uncle Fred—he's dead now—asked his wife to learn him to cook. 'In case anything goes wrong,' he say, 'and you're upstairs,' he say, 'then I can look after you.' And he told Cynthia the same way. He say, 'You ought to teach Lennie how to do it', and Cynthia say, 'He can already do it.'

We've tried to bring Judith up right. If children were brought up in the knowledge of God and learning to help their parents and keep theirselves out of trouble, everything would be fine. There's always trouble at Sudbury Upper where Judith is now. People blame the parents for not bringing them up right. Not so many months back there was two boys that set fire to the school. Judith, she couldn't go to school for a fortnight to three weeks. Everything was charred and everywhere was black with soot and smoked out and everything. I reckon it'll take the rest of the year to rebuild. The chemistry lab was completely destroyed. The boys were caught. One was sent to Borstal, for three years I think, and the other one was sent to a Detention Centre. One of them admitted to setting fire to the school a year or so before *that*! He thought to himself, 'Haha! I'll do it twice!' Judy, she's hardly any trouble now. They caned her once at Sudbury Middle for throwing mud at a window but we don't complain to the teacher about anything like that—if children do wrong they deserve to be punished. I mean, Judy gets a smack from us occasionally just to check her, but nothing to bruise her. A lot of parents are rather severe in their hitting. The least little thing that go wrong nowadays and they don't stop to think about it first before they hit them.

A child should say Sir and Madam instead of calling people

by their christian names like children do today. I've even heard them calling their mother and father by their christian names which isn't right. I'll always remember my father telling me when I was small. You know, I was only three to four years old and I used to wear a little hat and I used to see his mistress and his boss and I always used to have to touch my hat to them and say 'Good evening, sir' or 'Good evening, madam'. And I think that's how it should be. Mr Rix doesn't like Sir or Madam. You just have to say 'Mr Rix' or 'Mrs Rix' and call their boys 'Trevor' and 'Peter'.

And children should be decently dressed and that—you know, not have their dresses and that silly short. When we used to go in to Sudbury, even married women and that, you know, they used to bend over like, you know, and you could see all what they'd got underneath. I think it's dangerous. I reckon the way girls have been dressing and that, it's brought about a lot of this rape business. And they should keep their clothes clean and change them every so often and bath twice or, at least, once a week. You're prevented from scabies, especially in the summer time when you get so hot and smelly.

Then there's good table manners and that. We were always brought up to say grace before meals. My father didn't go to church but he always brought me up to say grace: 'For what we are about to receive, Lord, make us truly thankful.' Judith has picked up a couple herself:

> Thank You for the world so sweet,
> Thank You for the food we eat,
> Thank You for the birds that sing,
> Thank You, Lord, for everything. Amen.

and

> Be present at our table, Lord.
> Be here and everywhere adored.
> Thy mercies bless, and grant that we
> May feast in paradise with Thee.

She wants to be a nurse when she grows up. Her hobby is helping old people. It doesn't matter how bad or ill they are, she'll go and see after them. She'll help anybody, for love like. If they've got arthritis or anything, it don't worry her. She'll go and visit her Uncle Stan and get the tea ready, and if he ain't made his bed she'll make it for him. She even helped in a house where my wife used to work in Bridge Street. She also likes watching television, she'll watch it nearly all afternoon for cricket and football. She's crazy on football. We get to arguing, us two. She supports Ipswich Town and I pretend I support Norwich just for fun. You always know when Ipswich have lost because she comes through into the kitchen with a face as long as a wet week. She loves watching *Starsky and Hutch* and all the horror and police things like I do. Some children see these things on the telly and think they can do the same and kill somebody: they think it really happens. We don't take it seriously. We look at it and that's as far as it goes.

There are mothers and fathers who have been sent to prison because they have no thought for their child and have no thought for God or Jesus. I've read of cases where they get a cigarette end and burn them on the buttocks and pour hot water over them. There've been some who've been charged with the murder of the child. The Social Services and the Welfare and that, they're supposed to see after these things but they don't seem to bother a lot about it. There's one young welfare woman, Mrs Taylor from Bildeston, she's been round to see us and that, and helped us with Judy at school and that, and that's how, you know, I think it ought to be. They seem to think at Sudbury Upper that Judy can't get on, but she gets on very well—*we* think she do at any rate. We had an up and downer with her housemaster, Mr ——. He wanted to put her in a smaller school where there's only four or five to a class. We didn't agree because she was quite happy at Sudbury Upper and she's got lots of friends there. So we fought it, and Mrs Taylor helped us. She had to go and see a psychologist at St Leonard's Hospital, Sudbury, and tell him and Mrs Baker, another social worker, about the family home, and he could find nothing wrong at all, he wanted to know what the housemaster was talking about. So they let her stop.

Like myself, Judy's a slow learner. I'm a terrible writer and she takes after me for writing. But she's a better scholar than I ever was—she can do Maths! And she reads at the Mission Hall and reads well. Last November, Mr Robin Williams come from Bury St Edmunds and he let her go up with him to give out the hymns, and whenever my wife or myself is taking over she reads a lesson.

Judy started school at Sudbury Infants when she was five. I never started school until I was six. My hands weren't formed properly till then; there weren't no bone hardly, they were all gristle. To get using my hands properly I used to have to help my Mum wash up and do odd jobs about the house. And I never walked until I was three. We got a bit worried about Judith's walking too. She didn't walk till she was four and then she went off all at once. We were sitting down at the table, Mother and I, and she was on the floor, and all at once she stood up and walked across the room all on her own. Really wonderful! All at once she just sort of gained confidence in herself, I suppose. The wife say, 'Have a look, Dad!', she say. 'The child's walking!' We was very concerned. The doctors told us not to worry. They said, 'She'll walk when she's ready.' She was talking but she was backward in walking, just like I was. I used to crawl about quick as lightning—my Dad used to laugh at me the way I used to get over the steps—but I wouldn't walk. What my Mum used to do, she used to say to me, 'Come on, Lennie. We'll go and get this pretty flower.' That's how she got me to walk.

Chapter Four

I was born in a caravan on Boxford Recreation Ground on the 17th of August, 1930. My father, he was a travelling showman on the roundabouts and side-shows with Bert Stock's Fair. My mother used to travel around with the same fair. She was on the stalls—Throw a Penny, the coconut shies and pitching the ball in the bucket. In fact, I never knew my mother, not at all, because, you see, she died when I was three weeks old, she died with tuberculosis. She was twenty-seven when she died, and he was in his early thirties. They'd only been married a year. I was born in a caravan and she died in the same caravan in Boxford. The doctor was called and he said, 'There's nothing I can do for her.' Medicines weren't so far advanced then as what they are now for T.B. My father had to bring me up on Nestlé's milk. In the end, my mother's sister and my mother's brother—Aunt Elsie and Uncle Private Bowers—took me in. They lived at No. 22, Ellis Street, Boxford, and brought me up till I was the age of three. She's still alive but he died about twenty years ago. He was a farmworker, traving and looking after horses, and he used to walk four miles to work and four miles home though he had a double hernia. He'd always sit and have his meals by the open range with his hat on. A nice old boy he was.

My father carried on travelling—Bury, Colchester, Chelmsford, and all over the place: he used to go in Essex and everywhere. The caravans had big horses, shire horses, to pull them and all the machinery was steam-driven. He carried on for three years, then he met Flo, my step-mother what it is now, in the village of Nayland. She was down at the fair and they got talking and they went out together and that, and her father said, 'If you want to marry my daughter, you'll have to pack up travelling around with the fair.' So he said all right, he would do and he looked around—he had no experience on the farms or anything—and he got a job as a cowman at Dedham. His wages were twenty-seven shillings a week, seven days a week, and out of that he had to pay six shillings a week rent for the cottage. It was a tied cottage but he had to pay a rent. Aunt Elsie didn't want me to go when my father come to take me away. She threw some plates at him.

My step-mother when she was young used to work in service as a kitchen maid, peeling vegetables and that at Assington Hall just through Newton. Of course she's old now, but she used to be a nice looking woman, not very tall, on the thin side with glasses. She lives at Newton, all alone in a Council house—No. 10, Airey Houses, Assington Road, Newton. We visit her when we can, but it's a difficult job to get over from here in Alpheton. There's hardly no bus service. We did go over once by taxi three years or so back, but that cost nearly six pound return. I saw her last year in Sudbury on The Market Hill. She knows the situation. We write letters. I write once in a blue moon because I'm a poor letter writer, but Judith, she'll write two or three times a year. My Aunt Elsie, she lives in Boxford in a place where they've flatlets for old people with a warden to watch over them day and night. The last I saw her was in Sudbury four or five years back. She was still cutting about as sprightly as ever and she was getting on for ninety. I don't write to her—I ain't sure of the address. The warden knows my address. If anything happens to her, everything comes to me. I'm the only one that belongs to her now.

My father died of hardening of the arteries on March the 15th, I think, 1974. The funeral was at Newton. My step-mother went against his wishes—he wanted to be cremated instead of buried. My two step-sisters, Eileen and May, were crying more than what I was. When I started going with my wife he threatened to burn the bible because she was a preacher. He didn't approve of the marriage. He come round in the end and said it was all right, but he wouldn't ever come to hear her preach. He never entered a church hardly, except when he married, yet he had a crucifix tattooed on his chest as a young man in the navy. He was tattooed all on his arms as well—all different badges and that, and horses and his wife, my real mother, Ruth, with her name underneath. He was seventy-four, I was forty-four and I'd started working for Mr Rix. He'd retired but he was doing odd jobs, a bit of gardening and that for an Austrian near where he lived at Newton Green. He just went out to the Agricultural Show at Hadleigh and came home and died. His own father died of cancer of the throat through smoking a pipe. He used to smoke two ounces a day. It choked him to death in the finish. It was horrible to see because all the cancer roots grew out of his mouth.

He was a bit of a lad in his time, my father. He used to have a dog when he was a boy and somehow it used to slide up on its own to the butcher's shop and come back with a joint of meat in its mouth or two or three pound of sausages. There was twelve children in the family. He used to tell us that you'd have two rounds of dry bread put round your plate for breakfast and that'd be all you'd get and you daren't ask for more. They went to school with paper bags wrapped round their feet for socks and shoes, and all they had for dinner was the piece of bread and dripping what they took. At night they just had a piece of bread and butter and jam. His father worked in the Harwich dockyards and all the children had to be in bed by the time he got home at six o'clock. His mother asked his brother Alf to go to the shop and when he said, 'I shan't!' she kicked him from the top to the bottom of the stairs. She was very strict. She stood over six foot tall and weighed fifteen stone. She died when he was fourteen and he always did say that, for some time after she died, she opened his bedroom door and said, 'Goodnight, boy!' every night. When she was alive she used to be a sleepwalker. She used to get up, come downstairs, unlock the door and walk round the Harwich Quay. There weren't no railing or anything to stop anybody falling in, but she never did and the police used to follow her around wherever she went to see if she was all right. They never touched her or anything, just saw her back into the house again. A policeman told my grandfather, he say, 'Do you know the best thing to stop that?' So he say, 'No. I don't know what to do.' So the policeman say, 'You want to stick a bath of cold water at the bottom of the stairs.' So, as she came down the stairs, you see, she stepped into this bath of cold water and it woke her up and she never did sleepwalk no more.

When his mother died, he said he was older than he was and joined up in the navy. I reckon he was very nearly six foot; I'm about five foot eight. He was very long on the leg. He had a thirty-four to thirty-five inch leg and mine's only twenty-nine. He left the navy then and joined the army over in Ireland for what they called The Sinn Fein Stunt. You had to be very careful. If an Irish girl was caught talking to one of the English soldiers, all her hair was shaved off. There was a corporal, you know, he tried to be more than he was. My father and a mate of his were sitting in the canteen drinking beer, and this corporal come round and called out 'Time!' and my father said, 'No, it ain't!' and punched him on the chin and knocked him right out. They gave him a hundred and some odd days for that. He said to the corporal, 'When I come back I'll shoot you, you B!' He had to go on board a ship to get to the glasshouse and he demanded that they should take his handcuffs off because aboard ship you shouldn't be handcuffed in case the ship go down. They did eventually take them off and, when he was released, he came back to the camp where he'd been before and asked about the corporal but he'd completely disappeared. And do you know what happened? They made *him* a corporal because he'd stuck out for his rights. But he weren't as violent as what I was: he never struck his wife. My step-mother used to have the occasional tiff with him and that was that.

After I was taken away from my Aunt Elsie and we went to live in the village of Dedham, half past four to five o'clock time, tea time, I used to toodlefoot across the fields to meet my father, and my step-mother was scared stiff because there was a pond near the farm and she was afraid I'd fall in. Once I went out to the kitchen to wash up for her and I moved the candle somehow—there was oil lamps and candles, of course, in those days—and I set fire to the curtains. My father ripped them down and threw them out in the garden and damped them down with water.

Dedham Church of England School, that's the first school I started at. Then my father went to Layer Marney so I went to Layer Marney School when I was seven or eight. We lived in one of the rent-free Coronation Cottages built during the old King George's coronation. Then we moved to a cottage in Halstead. At the school there I was in the school band. We used to play for the parents—*Polly Wolly Doodle* and suchlike, all the old songs, *Bobbie Bobbie Shafto, My Charming Billy-Boy*. I played the cymbals. Then we moved back to Dedham again to another farm and then to Tendring Hall, Stoke by Nayland. We were down there the biggest part of the war years. I went to Nayland School and I was a terror.

Stoke by Nayland's in Suffolk. Dedham's in Essex. Layer Marney's in Essex. Halstead's in Essex. Boxford where I was born, that comes under Suffolk but the postmark is Essex, so when I wrote to my Aunt Elsie where she used to live—No.

22, Ellis Street, Boxford—I had to put Near Colchester, Essex, though it was in Suffolk. Essex schools are more stricter. If you stayed away from school they'd soon be after you in Essex. People were always coming after my mother and she had to get a special form from the doctor to say why I didn't go to school. They call us 'silly Suffolk', I don't really know why—whether it's because we do daft things or talk peculiar or what! But I know why they call the people in Essex 'Essex calf'. The legend is they found a calf with its head through a five-barred gate and they didn't know what to do so they cut the head off.

At Tendring Hall Farm my father was cowman for Mr G. Wear. Tendring Hall was a huge hall with about a hundred acres of woodland, grass and that. It was handed over to the troops during the war. As schoolchildren I and my two step-sisters, Eileen and May—I weren't much more than eleven or twelve—we used to go up from the farm to the village at Stoke by Nayland to do the shopping. The soldiers standing at the pole across the dirt road leading into the camp and the farm used to call out, 'Who goes there?! Friend or foe?!' We carried identity cards so we'd just show them the identity cards and they'd let us go through. After the troops went away there was German prisoners of war come there. First of all it was the Italian prisoners, then, after that, the German prisoners came, after the Italians went away. There were guards but they could roam about where they liked, you know, in the area. None of them escaped.

We had an evacuee from Harwich stay with us for three years. He was the same age as myself. We used to climb up the straw stacks and slide down and we got a good spanking from Mr H. Barley, the shepherd, for chasing the sheep. This evacuee would tease the cockerel my father had in the run with the hens. One day my father said, 'I'll stop you at that game, my boy!' and he opened the chicken-run gate and the cockerel came out and chased him the hundred yard up into the wood and back again! He never teased it no more.

We went to Nayland and bought rod, reel, line, float, hooks and sinkers to go fishing for roach and perch in the stream on the farm. I fell in once. And we made an eel trap. There was a weir, you see, and we made a big box with little holes so the water could get out, and we fixed it over the weir so the water rushed into the box. And every two or three days we went to get the eels—they was two to three foot long sometimes—and took them home and fried them for breakfast and tea. Freshwater eels are very delicious. They go to the sea to spawn and come back again. You can't grip an eel in your hand, it wriggles out. To hold it you must have two fingers under its body and one over the top. We used to collect moorhens' eggs and eat them too. They're very rich. Moorhens used to be killed. Farmers reckoned they were a menace to the crops and pick ducklings' eyes out. Now they're protected. They reckon they're becoming extinct.

I can't be a blood donor because I had yellow jaundice in the war when I was still at Nayland School. I tried. They thanked me for wanting to be one but said there and then, 'You're immune to another attack yourself, but your blood given to someone else could have drastic results.' I was at home from school six weeks. Your skin goes yellow. You first notice it under your throat. The yellow stuff comes off your skin onto the sheets. The doctor come out and tell me I'd got yellow jaundice. You're laid on white sheets and they look yellow—but it all washes out. You weren't allowed to eat nothing. All you had was milk to drink or water to drink. Then gradually you come on and you had the white of an egg beat up. You know, when you was really queer you went delirious. I kept saying there was somebody in the room. 'Mum! Mum!' I kept calling. 'There's a man standing by my bed!' She used to come up and say, 'There ain't nobody here!' It was an awful complaint. I was thirteen, I suppose. I went back to school and I said to a boy—just looked at him, we were playing together—I say, 'Boy,' I say, 'you've got jaundice coming!' He was all yellow round the front of the neck. I went and told the headmaster, Swinner, and he come and sent him straight home. And that was what it was.

I had Swinner for two years. It was girls and boys mixed and there were between twenty and thirty of us in a class. Before Swinner I had Mrs Backhouse. She was a horrible old dear. You know, she'd send you up to Swinner for the cane for larking about laughing and the least little things. She died a few years back. When I was working at Brundon I see her down in Sudbury and spoke to her. She didn't know who I was. I say, 'Do you remember the little terror Mills at school?' She burst out laughing. 'Oh,' she say, 'I know who you are now! You *used* to be a little terror and all!'

Before Mrs Backhouse I had Mr Taylor. There used to be a gang of us and we used to annoy him. If he caned a boy we all used to sit there and go zzzzzzz. He used to give us three on each hand. The boy what sat next to me got the cane one day and he come back and say, 'He's not a bad old chap, is he?' and I burst out laughing and *I* had to go out and get the cane then! Six of the best. 'Mills! Come out *he-yarrh*! I will not *have* a boy laughing when I cane another boy!' One day I was dared to go in to school when it was break-time. They say, 'Len, I dare you to go in to school and put the cane on the fire!' So I goes marching in the school, gets the cane out of the cupboard, snaps it in half and—there were combustion stoves in the classrooms then—lifted the lid up and just jammed it down. Come later in the morning Mr Taylor wanted the cane and he couldn't find it but in a few days he got another one from somewhere. He caned me one day because I never come the previous afternoon, I played truant. He say to me, 'Well, Mills,' he say, 'why weren't you at school yesterday afternoon?' I say, 'I didn't feel very well, sir.' I was just playing about round the river. I was a complete dare devil.

When we'd packed, just before we finished school, we used to have to put the chairs on top of the desks. I go in there one day and knocked the lot off. Another time a couple of us were playing about with the inkwells and Swinner caught us. You know what he done to us? He sent us down to the Infants! We stood in front of the class of infants while they were all laughing at us: 'La la titty babies playing with the inkwells!' We just stood there laughing too. And of course we used to do some roaring with laughing when we had gas mask drill. You'd get your gas masks on and you'd start breathing and they'd go—[long wet Chaucerian sound. Ed.]

We used to get *severely* caned sometimes. We got it across the backside once for turning the girls upside-down. There used to be three or four of us, you know, and we used to hang them upside-down so their dress fell up, you see, and we smacked their backsides. One girl was frightened and she went and told Swinner, and he shouted at us, 'Mills! Hills! Cansdale! and Wyles! Come to my room please! . . . What have you been doing?!' The girl's name was Maureen and she was there. 'What have they been doing, Maureen?' 'They've been turning me upside-down, sir!' 'Right! Lean across that chair!' Whoosh. Whoosh. Whoosh. We came away with tears running down our faces. We weren't crying—you know, it just made our eyes water. But we was rubbing our bottoms. Before I left he say, 'I suppose today, Mills, you'll be chucking in the sponge.' I say, 'Yes. And a blooming good job too!' He'd a terrible job with us.

My best subject was drawing. I did some wonderful drawings—dogs and human persons and war scenes: aeroplanes, ships, tanks. And I used to be able to spell a fair bit and I was a good reader. And I was very good at English compositions—you know, you take a certain subject say you've been somewhere, and you write about it. But I couldn't get on with mathematics or anything like that. One day I just managed to get one sum right and Mr Taylor say, 'We'll have to get on to the B.B.C. to say that Mills has got a sum right!'

My mate, John, was called Pussy, I don't know why. I was called Oiky—that would be a nice title for the book! I used to get called Big Head as well. I've got rather a big head, you see. I want 7⅜ in a cap. If I go into a shop I've to ask for 7⅜ and sometimes they ain't got them! Then they started calling me Oiky. I've no idea why. They just said it, you know. I think, you know, it was probably to do with, you know, Eisenhower. You see he was called Oik.

I liked fighting. I was easily annoyed and I'd soon fly into anybody if they blamed me for something I didn't do. If somebody said, 'It's Len's fault. He's done it.' and I went out and got caned and it weren't me, I used to say, 'You wait till playtime, boy! I'll get you! I'll give you a hiding!' and I hit him with my fist. We used to get nose-bleeds, black eyes. We twisted our scarves round the hand and clumped eachother round the head. If the masters caught us they used to say, 'Put the boxing gloves on! If you want to fight, sort it out!' They had to get the police after me sometimes, I was taking it so bad. They told me if I didn't stop they'd send me away to a home. My father tried to get me away for corrective training but my step-mother stopped him. There used to be an old woman come out—she was some kind of doctor like—and she looked at the whole class and, as I was very backward like, I had to say 'Jack and Jill' and that to see how well I was progressing. Once when I was getting to leave school I stole six watches and took them to school and just give them away to the boys. I got into serious trouble over that. My step-mother come to the school and talked to Swinner about it, she said I was easily led. And this old woman, he told her what I'd done. Cor, she didn't half give me a dressing-down! She say, 'If you start stealing other people's things, they'll start stealing yours!'

My step-sister May was at the same school but in a lower

standard. Eileen was only a toddler. One would be about forty now I reckon. The other would be about thirty. I got on with May, the older of the two, more than I did with Eileen. Eileen was more haughty like, but May, she'd do anything for me and still do, she think the world of me now. We had a terrible job with Sister May during the war years, she was so nervous. Where we lived at Tendring Hall we was bang slap in the middle of four aerodromes and there was bombs going off all round us. When the air-raid sirens went, we got up and went down the dug-out made for us down on the farm. About twenty of us used to go in there and, as soon as the siren went, May used to go really frantic, she marched out and called to our next door neighbour, 'Come on, Mrs Humphrey! Come on, Mrs Humphrey! Jerry's about! Jerry's about!' May and Eileen and me, we were the only children on the farm. We'd go down into the dug-out three or four times a week sometimes—eleven, twelve o'clock at night for an hour or so. It was about twenty yards from the house and all the neighbours and that would go in there and we'd have a cup of tea. May cried and cried. I weren't worried myself. Being a complete dare devil I used to like staying outside to stand and watch. But my father always made me go inside.

We had a mock raid sometimes at school. Somebody'd shout 'Air raid!' and make out like that aeroplanes were going over and bombs dropping, and we had to dive underneath the desks. Once we saw a German plane shot down. We were out on the allotment and the anti-aircraft guns were firing at it and they brought it down as we stood watching. There was two fighters went up after him and the German he done a silly thing, he turned into the sun and couldn't see. We saw him go down in flames in a cornfield.

We used to have school gardens—the senior boys used to have a plot each. We looked after them ourselves and grew potatoes, carrots, onions, tomatoes . . . I loved it. I was the one that used to have the best tomatoes and that there was there. They used to quiz me what I'd do to them and I didn't do anything! The school supplied the plot and if you wanted anything off the plot you gave the school a few pence. One day I told Swinner my step-mother would like a few chrysanthemum cuttings, could I go and get some. He say, 'Let's have a look at the soles of your shoes before you go down!' to stop me, he thought, taking apples off the apple trees. It didn't make no difference because when we went down we used to take our shoes off. 'Been after the apples?' 'No, sir.' We used to go out with him once a week for a proper gardening lesson. No girls. The girls used to stay in and do needlework and that. If it was too wet to go on the garden the boys used to do woodwork. I couldn't get on with woodwork so I used to do needlework and knitting with the girls—cushion covers, scarves. I was good at that, I used to love it. There was a girl who used to sit beside me. Her name was Avril. The boys used to take the mickey. They used to call me 'Old cissy'. Another was June Bullock. We used to do our courting and that as we went home from school. I used to carry her satchel and she used to hold my hand. Nearly all the boys had girlfriends. We had some fun. We used to lay on the river bank kissing and cuddling. We were never told nothing about the facts of life, we found them out for ourselves. Any fool can do 'that'. When I was grown up and married, there were two—their names was Jean and Don—and he had to ask his mother and father how to do it *after they were married*! His father say, 'I'm not going to tell you. You can buy a book on the subject. If you can't do that,' he say, 'you *are* blooming daft!' It just comes naturally, don't it?

When I was at Nayland School—and afterwards—I used to breed rabbits on the farm, it was such a huge place. My father started me off like. He say, 'Now earn yourself a few extra shillings!' I used to have between thirty and forty of them in huts at one time—grey, black and white, ginger and white . . . I took them to the market at Colchester and sold them for fourteen shillings to a pound. Now they're more expensive!

My father kept dogs—collie dogs, pekinese. We had a dog once when we was at Dedham—a little terrier—and it used to sit and laugh at you. And if you got a chicken out, you used to say, 'Go and get that chicken, boy!' and he'd go and get that chicken and he'd hold it with his paw and lay his head on it till you got there! We bought it off some gipsies and I reckon that's how they used to get free chickens. In the end we exchanged it for a pekinese.

My father, he was always a bit of a lad. He liked acting the fool. During the First World War—in Egypt somewhere—he used to see after the mules for the gun carriages. They had one mule there and one of the chaps say to my Dad, 'Len,' he say, because my father's name was Len the same as mine, 'Len,' he say, 'I can't catch that mule!' So my father say, 'What you've got to do is call it an old bugger!' And my father showed him, he went out and called it an old bugger, and it chased him in the tent and everywhere! Everyone was standing round roaring with laughter and saying it must have understood him!

Once when I was thirteen or fourteen he went up Stoke by Nayland village dressed up as a woman. He had a coat on and a dress and a pair of woman's shoes, and put lipstick on, you know, and a pair of glasses to disguise his face, and covered his hair right up with a hat! He had old fashioned drawers on with lace on the bottom and kept pulling his dress up and showing them. Nobody knew him and he went into the village hall where there was a concert and still nobody knew him. People kept coming up to me and saying, 'Who's that woman sat there?' I say, 'I don't know. I've never seen her before. I suppose it might be someone over on holiday.' I'd difficulty keeping a straight face. He went and sat by the parson and said 'Good evening' to him and the parson kept calling him 'My dear'. Then all at once somebody recognised him so the parson looked at him and said, 'It's you, you bugger, isn't it?!'—he come right out with it. During the acts he went head over heels right along the whole length of the aisle between the chairs. Somersaults, cartwheels—he was very agile. I tried to do it myself and I couldn't blinking well get head over heels let alone anything else! My sister May cried in case he hurt hisself.

He was a sergeant in the Home Guard. He got up a tree one night and he heard a commanding officer saying to a group of privates, 'Where is Len? I can't see him nowhere. He ain't slipped off into the pub, have he?' My father shouted down, 'If you don't watch out together, I'll shoot you!' They stood there shaking.

He was stood on duty another night and he called out, 'Halt! Who goes there?' and this woman of the road called back, 'It's all right, my darlings, my dears! I've got my identity!' She was a funny lass. Sometimes she'd swear at you left right and centre, and another time she'd be right as ninepence, she'd chat with you and tell you all the diseases she'd had—measles, chicken pox . . . But if small boys were cheeky to her she'd say, 'Go and smack their ear for me!' What made her like that was because she was jilted. A chap jilted her and she just sort of took to roaming the roads and sleeping in churches. She must be getting in her eighties. She had to go to court, the early part of this year I think it was. There were some rose bushes beside a footpath and, of course, the chap shouldn't have put them there by rights so she pulled them up and threw them over the hedge. He took her to court over it. They had to keep telling her to keep quiet or else she'd be in contempt of court like for shouting. And as it began to get warmer she was taking off the sheets of newspaper she'd got wrapped round her body and laying them on the chair beside her. She had a solicitor and all, and got away with it. They reckon she's well-to-do and she's a lovely home and that in Sudbury. She'll stay at home and then, when the moon affects her, she'll go off wandering the roads again.

I would like to have been a doctor if I'd had the education. Even as a boy I always did take great interest in medical things. My mother used to have a book at home called 'The Family Doctor'. I was always reading that about different diseases—scarlet fever, small pox, you know. And a year or so ago there was that series on television called 'Your Life In Their Hands'. There weren't no chance at the schools like there is now, you see. Like where Judith goes now to the Sudbury Upper School—she's got every chance for different subjects. At the schools I went to there weren't no O Levels and A Levels and GCE. None of us went to university or colleges or anything. And there weren't no Careers Offices in those days, you had to take what employment you could. In 1949 or so I had a hernia operation and they gave me surgical instruments to clean up with methylated spirits—forceps, knives, tweezers, all different shapes and sizes of scissors, they used to bring me a whole trayful. Another job they gave me was to make swabs with a sort of bandage stuff. In hospital I've always taken a great interest in what was going on. Looking at persons who are injured or anything like that don't worry me at all, I've always gone and attended to them as best I could. When I was at Nayland School there was an American aeroplane that crashed near the school and the pilot stayed in the plane to avoid the village and got killed. If he hadn't struck a tree they reckon he'd have been all right. Some of us runned over to see if there was anything we could do. He was smashed to smithereens with bones sticking out of his back. Some of the boys runned away and some just stood there, but I dragged him clear of the plane. Another time, at Hadleigh, I was out that way helping move the harvest and a big Fortress come over. He'd been over to Germany and his engines had failed and he couldn't get over the bridge across the river and he went smack right into the bridge and, as the tail come up, it shot the rear gunner out and smashed him all up on the parapet of the bridge. Even the police wouldn't clear the mess off the brick wall. I said, 'Give us a shovel and I'll do it for you' and I put it all into a plastic bag.

Chapter Five

When I first left school I did odd jobs on the farm to help my mum and dad. The old builder at Nayland, William Deaves—he was Undertaker and Plumber as well—he used to see me trudging along with an old push-chair going up to my grandma's, you know, my step-mother's mother, with the washing I collected round the village. He see my father one day and he say, 'Humping washing about! Hasn't he got a job?' My father say, 'Not properly.' 'Well,' he say, 'do you think he'd like to come and work for *me*?' So I used to take his old cart up to the saw sheds—he had a steam engine in there to saw the wood—and I used to get the boards that were cut out ready for the coffins and take them back down to the workshop and help the carpenter make them up. I put the pitch and stuff in and helped line them with satin and I put the pillows in and lace rims at the top—they really looked lovely, like beds. We had to make one for a woman once. She weighed twenty-two stone. It was a really huge coffin. She was so heavy they wanted extra men to lift her. The boss asked, he say, 'Will you go along, boy, with them?' I say, 'Yes, I'll go' and I helped them lay her into the coffin as if she was being put to bed and then put it in the lorry and took her to the morgue to keep her fresh on an ice-slab till the time of the funeral. The relations and that were in the house but they hadn't got the room.

Then I used to go with the plumber to help him wipe the pipes and put the hemp round and put the nuts on, and if a boiler wanted draining I used to drain that as well. One day we had a bit of fun. The people were out of the house. We went and got the key from the housekeeper and there was a bottle inside that had some whisky in. We emptied that and then we flooded the floor with water from the boiler. The plumber say it were all my fault. I say, 'It weren't! You're the one that took the nut out of the boiler, *I* weren't!' I suppose you could say it were then that I started drinking, but it were at Newton that I drunk the most when I was working for Mr Oliver before I was married.

At Tendring Hall Farm, Willie Humphrey, the neighbour, he used to make home brewed beer. Cor, it was lovely that was! He'd buy the hops and use the barley off the farm. He used to have big old ten-gallon barrels full of it. It was better than what you could buy. You didn't want many glasses of it before you were drunk. You used to go round there—'Want a glass of beer, boy?' His daughter used to chase me around the farm with the dishcloth and wrap it round my face.

The first proper job I ever had on a farm was with Mr G. Page, Thorington Hall, Thorington Street, Stoke by Nayland. I went to the farm foreman and asked if he'd give me a job because I'd just left school. He said, 'Yes, certainly. When can you start?' and I told him, 'Right away!' He said, 'Right. Come and see me on Monday.' His name was Mr Britten. He was a tall thin man with a moustache, between forty and forty-five, a very good foreman. The first day he set me on to harrowing the field. He showed me how to harness the horse up and how to put it onto the harrows and just went across the field once with me and left me to it. The wages were about six pound a week when I started. I worked there for a month and he gave me ten shillings increase and that's where they stayed for the next four years.

The horse is my favourite animal of all. I always did like

horses. At Page's I used to have to walk the horses three miles to the smithy at Stoke by Nayland to be shod. I'd be out nearly all day. Mr David Meekins was the blacksmith, but the man who used to shoe the horses, his name was Mr Chapman. When you've got two horses, you go on the opposite side of the road so you face the on-coming traffic. You place the riderless horse nearest to the hedge. I got into trouble once. A motorcyclist nearly hit me. But it weren't my fault, I was in my rights. The police came out and the cyclist was going to do this, that and the other. The policeman say, 'There's nothing you can do,' he say, 'because the chap was in his rights.' He say, 'You look at your Highway Code. It'll tell you that.' I had one horse, you had to hang on for dear life! It could smell a pig lorry a mile away. It never did like pigs. It would gallop away even if you was in the middle of a field with a cart and all. You couldn't hold him, you just couldn't hold him. Another thing—a horse will never go past blood. Say you went to a stable and you left your horse outside and you smeared some blood on the doorpost, you wouldn't get in! I caught a rabbit once when I was carting mangles for the cattle. I run and caught this rabbit, held it up by the hind legs, give it a rabbit punch on the back of the neck, took it back to the horse and cart, and the horse bolted. The rabbit's nose, you see, was bleeding. The horseman say, 'Never take blood near a horse, boy. They always run and you'll never do nothing with them.'

The men at Page's used to start at five o'clock in the morning and work right through, after a break at nine for wittles,—in Suffolk we always say 'wittles' for 'breakfast'— till three o'clock in the afternoon. They'd leave off at three o'clock (twelve on Saturdays), take the horses home to the stable, take the harness off, feed them with oats and chaff and groom them down, turn them out on the meadow, and they'd finished for the day. I started at seven, not five, because I wasn't eighteen. But that two hours didn't matter because I was harrowing the corn in and I could do quicker than what the seed drill could. The seed drill had to stop every so often and fill up again, and I could keep going up and down.

To put the horse's collar on you have to have it turned upside down, put it over the horse's head and, as it's on the neck, turn it round and shove it back to the shoulders. You put the bridle on next. Then you put your breeches on—the saddle and the straps that come down over the hind parts and the girth going underneath the belly. Then you do up the strap from the saddle to the collar so the collar can't come forward, then you strap the girth onto the saddle. There's two wooden things called filberts fixed on the collar permanently and they've got the trace-chains on—you use short chains for a cart and long chains for harrowing and ploughing. The long chains are hooked onto the whippletree of the harrows when you get to the field—that's the short pole. The long pole that the harrows are chained to—you've either six or eight harrows—what they call the pommeltree. The whippletree is attached to the pommeltree. It's on a swivel chain so that it can swing about and let you turn the horse without turning on your harrows.

So I just set my harrows up and went up and down the fields all day long. There was a seed drill on the field with two horses and two men, one walking behind to keep an eye on the seed and the other at the side guiding the horses and keeping the marker wheel of the drill in the right place. I was harrowing behind the drill, covering the corn seed up. I used to thoroughly enjoy walking up and down the fields March-April time.

When the spring corn came through nice and green about two or three inches—that would be round April/May time—we rolled the fields to keep the ground down a bit firm and keep the moisture in. There were several thousand acres to do so the rolling lasted about six or seven weeks. Mr Page's whole estate had several farms and twenty horses and between twenty and thirty men. The rib-roll, about six foot long, heavy, it'd have to have two good strong fast-walking horses, shires, coal horses that used to pull coal up and down the streets in London—one in the shafts and one horse next to it on a trace-chain free for turning. Then it used to be horse-hoeing the sugar beet and the kale, keeping the weeds out between the rows. We had a thousand sheep and the kale was for the sheep in the winter months. I used to walk the horse up between two rows. You used to have to keep that horse dead in the middle, you mustn't step out at all, or you'd cut your seeds out.

That'd bring you nearly up to harvest, July-August time. Towards the end of cutting the corn with the binder and traving,—standing the sheaves up—eight sheaves to a trave, we used to stand round with sticks in the hand and catch rabbits. As the field got smaller the rabbits would run out and we used to chase them and kill them—one hit on the head, that's all they wanted. Grey rabbits. Wild rabbits are grey. Mr Kerridge, the butcher at Nayland, he used to take them from us for about two shillings each. Then I'd be stacking the corn at the top of the elevator. There'd be three of us stacking of it from seven o'clock in the morning till eight o'clock at night and next, after the fortnight's holiday in September, my job was to bag up the chaff for the bullocks and the horses in the winter, or I'd help cart the straw into the yards for the cattle and carry water in a water-butt to the troughs for the shepherd.

I did hedge-laying and muck-carting in the winter. For the muck-carting I had a tumbril, a two-wheel cart affair, horse-drawn. We worked in pairs. You put so much on a heap—about two barrow loads—, went eight yards, put another heap down, and you'd to do that all day long, twenty tumbril-loads a day before you left off work. You used a 'chrome', a long handled fork with three prongs bent over on the end of it. Gee up! Eight paces. Woah! I can remember the time when I was machine-gunned. I was going across a field with a horse and tumbril at about midday and three German planes came over and they machine-gunned us. The horse bolted. We lay flat in the tumbril and just let him go. We'd a terrible job to hold him afterwards.

I liked the hedging, laying the hedges. It's very nice laying the hedges in the winter time. It keeps you nice and warm. There's an art to it. I wouldn't be an expert at it myself but you'd get some old boys who've been on the land all their life till they're sixty; they can do it to a T. You lay a hedge in the opposite direction to the way you're going. You go along, you don't cut a twig right off, you make a cut in it with a hook so it splits, and bend it over and lay it flat about a foot or so from the ground and it stays there horizontal. It's still got sap in it and next season it'll be green and beautiful. To stop the twigs spring back we sometimes tied them down with a piece of wire until the wood struck; then the wire would rust away. You can cut some waste out so the hedge ain't too thick. When it grows up again all you've got to do is settle it with a shears to make it nice and tidy. You do it to get a flat-top hedge. You can't lay hedges that are too high, over about five foot. We used to do it right away along a field, hundreds of yards sometimes. It's wonderful the things you can do with rips, slashers, saws, sickles, scythes and hooks. But there's no hedge-laying about here now. We've no hedges. A lot of farmers have done away with hedges; you know, they're putting two or three fields into one so that there are right big fields instead of little fields. The birds ain't got nowhere to nest and there's no wind breaks. There used to be a hedge near Primrose Cottage on that hill as you go in to Melford after Bridge Street. When that hedge was cut down and we had the bad snow, it all drifted into the road and nobody could get through no way. In the fields it doesn't matter so much, but it do near the roads. We've had snow badly only once since I've been up here. It drifted into the lane so bad I'd to go down to the farm by the side of the field. The lane was blocked up; the pig lorry couldn't come for three weeks. Mr Rix was going to church one morning. I told him before he went out, I say, 'You won't go to church this morning, Mr Rix. It's drifting up on the lane.' He would have his headstrong way and go and, of course, before he could get his car back to the farm, he had to get the tractor out and I'd to help him dig his way back to the car to get it through. The only trouble you have with pigs in snowy weather is the water might freeze up but, touch wood, that didn't happen.

The sheep would be turned out onto the fields February, March time and they'd start lambing and the lambs and sheep would have huts to go in made of bales of straw and hurdles. Then the fields ploughed October, November, December, would be ploughed over again, ready for the spring drilling.

Wonderful experiences I've had on the land. The thrushes early in the morning and what they call the dawn chorus. Red sky at night, shepherds' delight—'Nice day tomorrow!' we used to say. Taking our haversacks out into the fields with us and hanging them on a tree somewhere in the shade . . . Nine o'clock we used to stop for wittles and sit down in the hedge for a half hour: if the weather was right we'd be out there even in the winter, and if it weren't there'd be a shepherd's hut with a fireplace in nearly every field. Half a loaf of bread with a hole cut in the middle and a ball of butter down the hole. Cutting lumps off the bread with our penknives. Onion and cheese. A flask of tea . . . I used to thoroughly enjoy it. Then home for dinner at three thirty—potatoes, peas, meat, rice pudding. Helping my father in the garden, digging and planting the potatoes, hoeing the weeds. Then cocoa and sweet digestive biscuits or cream crackers and a bit of cheese for supper before going to bed between nine and ten. I used to take a mangel home sometimes to make mangel wine. Mangel wine will soon put you on your back. My mother made no end of wines—rhubarb wine, parsnip wine, date wine, tea wine, pea wine, beetroot wine, blackcurrant wine, dandelion wine . . . That's very strong that is. One little glass of that and you're gone.

Every Sunday morning and night, and sometimes during the week if they had a choir practice, I went to the church at Nayland to pump the organ. There was two of us pumping it. The organist paid us six shillings a time each and the church warden gave us about three. We used to make noises at the choir girls for devilment. The choir mistress come after us once and told us to stop putting the choir girls off. They used to put their book down a bit and look at us and grin during the service. We'd no light to show us when to start pumping: you could hear a knock when the organist pressed one of the pedals or one of the keys down. You didn't get much rest; you could only stop when they had the bible readings and the prayers. My mother and father hardly ever went to church, but they never stopped me going to pump the organ—or to Sunday School. I went to Sunday School with my two step-sisters when I was younger.

I'd to leave Page's at the end of four years because my father moved to, I was helping out at . . . oh, it's come to me now,—my father moved so many times!—Mr Crag's at Alresford in Essex near Brightlingsea. Mr Crag was a very religious man; it wouldn't do to swear where he was; he'd go to chapel every Sunday. A bloke one day—his name was Harry—he broke some posts down with a tractor. It made me wild because some of the cows got out. I said to Mr Crag—I weren't a Christian then—, 'Godaheck! They break hell!' He said, 'Sh, sh, sh, sh! Tut, tut, tut, tut! Don't talk like that!' I was still earning £6 to £7 a week. My father was getting £12 or £13 as a cowman. He was a man, you see. I weren't; I weren't twenty-one. You didn't get a man's wages then till you was twenty-one. Now it's eighteen.

We were living in an old farmhouse that had nine

bedrooms, Plumpton's Farm. I was able to go on breeding rabbits, I'd rabbit hutches about there all ways. On my day off, Saturdays, well, I used to put them on Mr Crag's own milk lorry when it come to pick the churns up, and take them in to Colchester to sell them and come back on the bus.

We had a chimney fire one day and there weren't no fire! It was an old chimney, you know, and it had ledges inside, you know, and there was some soot on one of these ledges and we had a fire previously and this soot was just smouldering. We phoned the Governor up—he lived at Lexden—and we told him, 'We need the fire brigade!' There was fire engines coming down in all directions. They had to rip all the fireplace out to get at it.

I had a pal to go about with—Peter. After I'd finished helping my father out with the cows I used to go out on the land with Peter, helping with the sugar beet and the harvest. He was a tractor driver, a little bit younger than I was. We had the day off and went to the Suffolk Show near Colchester. Crag's was the only time I went to the Suffolk Show. It used to be at different places every year but it's been permanent this last two or three years in Ipswich. Some farmers let all their workers go. Only over there, with Crag, we went; he let us have a day off to go. Peter and I biked it and turned right instead of going straight on. A policeman was in the middle of the road and we come back again and the policeman, he say, 'You'll soon know where you're going, won't you?!' I said to him, I say, 'You want to sign-post it right!' and he just laughed. The beer tents and the food tents was extremely expensive. But we had cards, you know, same as like Doe's of Sudbury or Eastern Tractors or Barclay Tractors, their representatives used to give the farmers so many cards and, if their stand was at the show, they used to give us a card, the farmer did, and we could go into that firm's tent and have a meal and that free of charge. Peter and I had a Doe's card—

they're tractor specialists. We had roast beef, potatoes, green peas, soup of the day first. Then we had some beer.

We belonged to the Transport and General Workers' Union when we was at Alresford. They had an annual outing for the members of Alresford and Wivehoe and that and we went to Southend for the day. We had some nice fun. There were crates of beer on the back of the bus, you know, and we went to the Kursaal, you know, the amusement park and all that. One of the chaps what was with us, he wore a cap, you know, and he went on the scenic railway,—it's one of the biggest scenic railways—he went on that and lost his hat and nobody found it any more.

My father only stayed a year with Mr Crag. He was very hot tempered my father. If anything upset him he was off; if the Governor said the cows weren't giving enough milk, anything like that, he'd have his say and off he'd go. We went to Ramsey where he worked for about a year for a Mr Cresswell. He looked after the cows at South Hall where we lived in a brand new tied cottage, and I'd to bike about two miles before I got to my job, milking full time, at North Hall. It was there where I got my hernia. I just slipped in the cowshed and that was that. I was in hospital six weeks and three months at home. The Union helped me a lot over that. It was an injury at work, you see, and the Governor, he didn't want to pay compensation. The Union took him to court and he had to, he had to pay me twenty-five shillings a week compensation till I went back to work and part of my £6 a week pay as well.

Ramsey weren't much cop. You had to go right down to Dovercourt, a seaside place with Woolworth's, Marks and Spencer's and everything. I used to go paddling, take my shoes and socks off, roll up my trousers. And I liked the rifle range in the amusement park. I was a good shot. You got five hits for a shilling and won a prize if you got so many points. I once won a glass. It was an ordinary drinking glass to look at but when you tipped it up into the light you could see a naked woman inside on the bottom.

Next we moved to Newton and worked at Mr Wade's at Butler's Hall, a dairy farm with about forty cows on about two hundred and fifty acres. Mr Wade was only young, twenty five to thirty. While I was there he got married. She was a farmer's daughter from Boxford, a very nice person. He didn't understand anything about much. His father used to run the farm, then he got the gun and shot himself; they found him dead one day in the horses' stable.

I lived with my step-mother and father and two step-sisters in a council house as there weren't no house with the job. Mr Wade applied for a house for a farm worker but the council wouldn't let him have one, so he paid half the rent of this council house with a big garden and we paid the other half, about ten shillings a week. The wages was much the same as before but we left the union. They used to keep coming after you at your house for the subscriptions, three shillings a month. You didn't know where you were or nothing else. The secretary kept coming. He come one week and then the next week he'd come after some more after you'd already paid. No end of farm workers chucked it in.

My father and myself worked together. He was Leonard Edward and I'm Leonard Arthur so they used to call me George. Five o'clock in the morning I went out in the meadow, took the cows home, drove them along with sticks and a Scotch collie, put them into the yard, put eight at a time into the cowshed to milk, fed them, washed the udders with water, stripped a little bit of milk onto a fore-cup to see if there were any illnesses like mastitis. Mastitis is when the milk has got lumps in; then it's not fit for human consumption and goes to the calves. If a cow had mastitis I said, 'Cow wrong here, Dad!' We used to have to get a tube of penicillin and squeeze it up the teat. My father used to milk the cows by machine and I used to go behind and when the cups were taken off the teats I sat down on the stool and stripped them, stripped the last drop out with my hands. We'd be finished milking about eight o'clock, and I turned the cows out onto the meadow and then we used to go home for an hour and have breakfast, then came back, washed out the machines, the buckets, the churns, mucked out the cowshed. Then it would be dinner time, one o'clock. Come back two o'clock, went down the fields again, got the cows home, same procedure again till five o'clock at night. Then you were finished unless there was any calving—then you used to come back and see if they was all right. We worked six days a week, a different day off every week. Once a week I went out with boyfriends to the pictures at the Gainsborough or The County in Sudbury. The County's been pulled down. We had some laughs. We used to sit in the balcony for about one and threepence and buy sweets and ice-cream. Otherwise I'd stay indoors and help with the garden. On your day off a relief chap would come in. When my dad had a day off I did the machines and the relief would do the stripping. Same when I was off—he done all the stripping, the relief man.

When I was very young at Tendring Hall, Stoke by Nayland, I used to go to The Gaumont, I think, in Colchester with my two young sisters and my father. I remember the first time we went. The film was something to do with some natives. You know, Zulus and that dancing about and carrying babies on their backs. A white man whipped one of the men, you know, because he'd done something wrong. My sister May sat there on her chair and my father looked at her and say, 'What the heck are you doing up *there*, girl?!' She didn't realise that the chair had got to come down!

I stayed with Mr Wade for about three years at the same wages. My father left before me and went to look after poultry for a Mr Smith at Leavenheath. He was getting on and his hands packed up. Doing hand-milking for so long before Wade's, the muscles of his arms and fingers got so weak he couldn't use his hands hardly. I stayed on for a little while and a new bloke come in. We called him Tom and, you know, he wanted everything done like *his* way. We'd been doing it our way like, and he wanted to do it his way—three-times milking. He wanted to milk at five and at three and then pick out a dozen or so cows that give plenty of milk and give them extra food and milk them again between eight and nine o'clock at night. It's too much on the cow, I reckon. There were several farms around who were doing of it. I done it for a time and then I told him I wanted to hand my notice in to Mr Wade. I could have gone on the land but I didn't want to because if anything went wrong he'd have wanted me back there in the cows again. Mr Wade didn't think three-times milking was cruel.

I always did love animals. It grieves my heart to see them being ill-treated. There was one farm I was on, the pigs weren't getting enough food. You see, you can overfeed pigs. When you're sending the cutters and baconers and porkers to the slaughterhouse they mustn't be too fat, they must only have so many millimetres of fat on. If you've got a millimetre over, they're not what's called 'Q lean', they're into the next grade. If they're Q lean, you get an extra two to three pound in money per pig. But this man wasn't even giving them enough food to keep them comfortable. When a pig has had plenty to eat it'll lie down nearly all day. These started to eat the insides out of each other, they started to bite one another's tails. They looked a sorry sight, some of them. The farm-workers all had an up and downer over it. We said if he didn't feed them and look after them better and that, you know, we'd get somebody else to come out and see to it. The whole staff turned on him and they turned on the pigman—he was a boss's man, you know. There was a public right of way, a footpath, right through the farm. People used to hear the pigs squealing and calling out; they used to ask what was wrong. Well, you had to tell them the truth, you couldn't hide nothing; if they went round and found them themselves you was in trouble yourself. So the pigs got more food.

Not up here at Mr Rix's but another farm we went to visit once to see about the wet feeding, the farmer there, he'd got just a small square area and about twenty to thirty pigs, and they were rolling all over the top of one another, there weren't no room at all. I like to see animals have plenty of room to move about because when you've got animals and that all hemmed up tight together you get injuries and you get disease. I like to see animals free. You get some farrowing crates where the sows are penned in a whole five weeks when they have their piglets. At least with Mr Rix they can move backwards and forwards a bit if they want to. One thing I entirely disagree with is battery hens, hens in cages all day long. Their eggs are forced out of them; some of them lay two or three eggs a day. This is not right and the eggs ain't the same in taste as the free range. And I don't like factory farming. Calves are born and they're took straight away from the mother and they're put in entire darkness for three to six months, then they're killed at the butcher's right away and go for veal. They're all in such a small area, everythings crowded right tight and they haven't got any room to move at all. Oh yes, there's a terrible lot of cruelty to animals these days. Up at Ashen, just the other side of Clare, there's somebody found a cat and it was crucified to a tree. Recently, too, there was another one at Bury St Edmunds. That was in the Abbey Gardens. One of the gardeners heard some youths making a noise and he shouted at them and they runned away and he went over to investigate and he found this kitten crucified with one of its legs broke and it was still alive. There was a picture of it in *The Free Press*. I just don't know why they do it.

One thing I'll tell you, I never give to the RSPCA. When we lived at Brundon, the Governor, the young Mr Norman, wanted cats destroyed. It was bitterly cold and, poor dears, he set traps for them with fish in and, poor dears, as they went in to grab the fish like, well that released a lever and a door slammed shut behind and they couldn't get out any more. Poor dears, they were crying with cold and absolutely wild when we went there in the morning. The man from the RSPCA come the next morning to destroy them—they were his cages, you see. He had a noose on the end of a pole and the rope run through a sort of hollow pipe affair and he'd drop his noose over the cat's neck and pull it tight and take it into another cage, then take it away and destroy it. We reckoned that was cruel. My wife had a real up and downer with the man, she went at him left right and centre. She choked him off like, you know, she say, 'The RSPCA should have an I for Infliction not a P for Prevention!' The man took no notice. He set the cages again and this time the wife and I, we kicked them all over, sprung them so the cats couldn't get in. He come the next morning and the Governor come after us but we pushed a few bales of straw down on purpose and we say, 'You can see what happened, can't you? Some of the bales fell down on them,' and my wife gave the man from the RSPCA another dressing down so he say to the Governor, he say, 'I ain't coming down here no more! Especially I ain't vooming down where that woman is!'

And my wife told me there's another RSPCA man. His wife died of cancer, and all the stray dogs and cats about, he's capturing them and sending them to research centres for cancer and that to see if they can cure it. I said to myself, I say, 'Why don't he offer hisself instead of letting animals suffer?' If they wanted my body for research and I'd have died, they could have had it.

Chapter Six

I left Wade's and went to see Mr Campbell, Mr Oliver's farm manager at Newton, and asked could he give me a job. He said I could go on the land, tractor driving. I done tractor driving for him for two years. One of the other tractor drivers—Bill, my brother-in-law—showed me what to do the very first week. In those days the tractors had to be started up on petrol. You cranked the starting handle, put your choke how you wanted it, turned the tap to switch the petrol off, then the paraffin run into the carburettor. You had to be very careful when you started them up because, the old tractors, they kick, you can easily break your wrist if you don't hold the starting handle right. You mustn't put your thumb, same as if you're holding a walking-stick, with your hand right round it, you've got to put your thumb over the top to stop it flying out of your hand. Round about 57/58 we switched over to diesel tractors. You didn't have to crank them up. You had a key and you just turned it and the tractor started.

To start with I was put harrowing and rolling and cutting the sugar beet. The sugar beet was in the winter time. What we used to do was take eight rows, all piece work, so much a hundred yards. The sugar beet lifter, a sort of plough affair, used to go between the rows and pick the beet up and leave them there and we'd come behind on foot and knock them together to get the dirt off and lay them into rows, four rows one side with the tops laying outwards, four rows the other side. Then, after we'd done so many yards like, we used to go back again and top them with a sugar beet hook and put them into heaps and the trailer and tractor come behind and we put them into the trailer. The leaves stayed on the field and after the sugar beet had been carted off we used to put an electric fence up and the cows used to come and eat them.

I started drinking when I left school but it were when I was working for Oliver at Newton that I drunk the most. I used to go in to The Saracen's Head or The Case Is Altered about seven o'clock and stay there till I got kicked out at ten o'clock. I used to love playing darts, you see, and I seemed to play better when I'd had a few drinks than what I did before. I belonged to The Saracen's Head Dart Team. The Saracen's Head Dart Team and The Case Is Altered Dart Team, the two teams would compete against each other once a week. It would be a different public house every week like, sometimes it would be a public house in Melford, sometimes it would be Acton or somewhere like that. I'd eat a hunk of bread and a hunk of cheese and some pickled onions and spend almost all the rest of my wages on drink and cigarettes. One night I got seriously drunk. I was drinking cider and then I went right on to whisky. The funny part about it was I rode my bike home as right as ninepence. But when I got to bed and started to get warm and that the ceiling started spinning round and come right down on top of me and I made a terrible mess everywhere.

I drunk small browns mostly. I didn't care for the beer up at The Saracen's Head—it was Tolly. The beer at The Case Is Altered was Ind Coope's and seemed to taste better. I got friendly with the landlord's wife, Mrs Brown. Everyone else was out at a darts match and she was there and I was there alone at night at The Case Is Altered sitting side by side of eachother in front of the fire drinking beer. 'You'll have another one before you go, won't you?' She kept buying me drinks. Then she put her arm around me. I was getting worried in case it went any further. But nothing got out of hand like, you know; it was all all right.

Christmas Day, Boxing Day, New Year's Day and all that I used to be most tipsy because the pubs stayed open longer. I was a bit wobbly like but I could always walk and ride the bike. When the Queen's coronation was, I went down to The Christopher in Sudbury, five boys together—Bill who married my sister Eileen, Arnold who married my sister May, Geoffrey (he's dead now, there was something wrong with his ear that killed him) and Lionel (he's alive but all on his own). The five of us used to go everywhere together, the pub, the pictures . . . We went in The Christopher that night and they'd got a special Coronation beer, small bottles about three shillings each, Ind Coope. We had three or four of them and we didn't want any more! Come out there and we was singing Roll Out The Barrel, Knees Up Mother Brown, rolling about the road, you know. We was having a rare happy time the five of us. We weren't violent, just merry like; the police saw us and never said anything. Then we had to struggle home on our bikes. *We* seemed to ride our bikes all right, but one poor bloke we met, we walked him to Newton and he say, 'Now put me on my bike,' he say. 'I shall be all right.' A few yards along the road, CRASH—off in the ditch!

I didn't stop drinking till after I met the wife. I don't drink at all now, I *can't* because of my operation. I don't say drink is a bad thing, it's just you can make a fool of yourself of it if you have too much. Before the operation I used to have a glass of beer occasionally in the house but I might go six months or a year without it.

Once or twice a year on a day off I used to go up with Lionel to London. Lionel Humm is his full name. We used to take the train from Sudbury to Liverpool Street and then go on the Underground to the West End. The first time we went up we went into a pub and I say, 'Let's have a game of darts' and, you know, we just got talking to the chaps in there. They wanted to know where we come from, you know, because we were two complete strangers. We told them and one of them say, 'It's nice to hear Suffolk people again' and they bought us drinks and that. There was about six of them and we'd had five or six pints by the time we'd finished. Then we went out in the streets again and we saw the old barrow boys and bought some fruit and one of them say to us, he say, 'You come from Suffolk, you two!' I say, 'Did you used to be in Suffolk then?' He say, 'Yes. It's so nice to hear the Suffolk language again.' We found the Londoners quite friendly. Then we had tea in some café and then we went to The Windmill where they had a comic show. Someone come out rattling tin cans. He was supposed to be drunk and he hadn't got a watch and he rattled these tin cans and someone opened the bedroom window and say, 'Do you know what time it is?! It's three o'clock in the morning!' 'Oh!' he say. 'I know the time now!!' There was women in the nude. Lionel was sat there and his mouth was wide open and his eyes standing a mile out. I was interested but I weren't like *he* was!

Whenever we went up we always went to The Windmill and got the last train back from Liverpool Street about twelve o'clock. These women were completely naked like, but you couldn't see much below their bosoms because they'd have these feather fans, they raised their fans quickly and then the lights just dimmed right down. There was all sorts in the audience, Japanese and all colours. They say, I don't know if it was true or not, they say if you write your name and the name of a certain girl on a bit of paper and give it to somebody to take round the back you can meet her after the show. Sometimes we went to Regent's Park Zoo. We used to have some rare fun there, seeing the lions and giraffes and our brothers, like we used to say, the monkeys. The lions would be roaring away there while the keeper with a long-handled fork copped the meat in to them. I didn't like them being kept in captivity, though. They tell you that an elephant never forgets. A keeper once lost his temper with an elephant and thrashed it, and he went away and he came back three years after as a visitor. And that elephant still knew him and chased him and if he hadn't got out of the way it would have killed him. When they're wild like that they'll pick you up in the trunk, throw you down and crush you with their foot. That's what they *say* they do. I've never seen it happen.

Mr Campbell, the farm manager at Oliver's, came to see me one morning. Somebody had left the cowshed so he said, 'Lennie, would you mind going in to the cows till I get somebody. I'll give you an extra quid a week.' That brought me up to eight or nine take-home pay a week. I said, 'No, I don't mind' and I went in the cowshed and he didn't want me to come out no more. In the end I said to Mr Campbell, 'How much longer are you going to be getting anybody in?' He say, 'You can stay.' I say, 'Oh, I didn't know. When I first started,' I say, 'you told me to come in till you got someone.' He say, 'You're a good bloke,' he say. 'You can stay there.' He'd seen the head cowman, you see, and he say, 'Is Len getting on with the cows, Ben?' So Ben say, 'All right,' he say. 'I don't want to wish for a better bloke. He's jolly good,' he say. 'He can stay in.'

You got a bonus for so many gallons over a hundred. I used to get four or five gallons over the hundred in the day and you got a shilling a gallon. It used to run into four or five pounds a month sometimes! There were six of us—Ben and five under him. When Ben had his day off, well *I* used to take over then, get up in the morning and get all the cows in ready for the other blokes when they come in ready to milk. I got a little extra for that and, when I took over during his fortnight's holiday, I got about another pound a week because I used to have to give the suckling calves their milk and there was more responsibility. Ben told me there was a Land Girl there one day during the war helping to milk the cows. She came in just an ordinary skirt and she was supposed to wear the uniform. One of the cowmen, Bill Armstrong it was, he was stripping a cow away and he was having a good butcher's round the cow at this girl bending over to put the machine on when the head Land Girl walked in on an inspection. She didn't half get a telling-off over it, she soon got told to keep her uniform on, her corduoroy breeches and that! Poor girls, they used to get hot in those uniforms but they had to wear them, winter and summer—breeches and khaki jumpers and blouses and hats with WLA on.

I met my wife when I was cowman at Oliver's. Mr Mitchell, her father, was once a Plymouth Brethren. With the Brethren you're only supposed to attend their churches but he didn't, he used to go round different churches, the Methodist churches and the Free churches and that, preaching. The Brethren, they didn't like it so they turned him out. In the end, Mr Rix, his employer and my present employer, who was 'oversight' of the Free Church Mission Hall, Bridge Street, resigned because he and his wife wanted to go to St John's Methodist Church, Sudbury, and my father-in-law as he is now, he took over till Cynthia became oversight in his place.

Before we were married I used to take Cynthia to Yarmouth. We had lovely times. We always used to buy our lunch—a bit of roast beef or roast lamb and roast potatoes. (We never used to take sandwiches; we got enough sandwiches and that at home.) Then we went on the beach and laid on the beach. The beach at Yarmouth is very long; it's a heck of a long beach before you can get to the sea. Once I get to the sea I always want to go in a boat, but the wife don't like the water, she sits on the beach waiting while I have the trip round the water. I can't swim but when Judith was old enough we used to go to Clacton, Walton or Felixstowe and we got some swimming trunks on, you know, and—oh we used to have some fun—I used to lay in the water and she'd lay there as well, not too far out so nothing could happen to her. Cynthia, she wouldn't come in, she was scared stiff.

We haven't been to the seaside for six or seven years. It's so expensive now to get anywhere travelling. I reckon to get to Clacton it would cost anything up to 70p each return, and Judith hasn't left school but she has to pay full fare. They have to pay full fare when they're eleven years old; it used to be fourteen. Seven years ago the fare to Clacton and back was five shillings. I should love to go to the seaside again one of these days. Mr Rix would give me the day off if I wanted it but up here in Alpheton, you see, you've difficulty to get the bus. We went to Walton once on a Sunday School outing. Cynthia's father organised it—that was before his stroke five years ago. Then Cynthia organised another one. We had a fair load that day. We brought our own dinner, and tea was provided out of the funds, you know, the Mission Room funds, the collections that we have every week. I believe that was four years ago, the first year we was up here. We went on the beach and the children, they liked the amusements. Judith went on the roundabout and the aeroplanes which go up and down. I like going in those chairs that swish round right quick. Cynthia won't come in. Then I like the scenic railway. You go up to the top slowly and once you get over the top you go whoosh. There are girls screaming.

When my wife and I were going together we went to Caxton Hall two or three times. Once a year, March time, they used to have a rally there for The Royal National Mission to Deep Sea Fishermen, I think it was called. Cynthia used to collect for it round the villages, you see, and occasionally a man used to come down and show us films of their work and that, how the trawlers get lost and lives are lost and injuries happen. Quite interesting. The first time, we found our own way there and everything. We went from Sudbury to Liverpool Street Station, then from Liverpool

Street Station to St James's Park. We had a time walking round, had our dinner and then we went to the meeting. We had to come out about half past eight time to catch the nine o'clock train. Mr Harvey, the area organiser, gave us the fare for a taxi to Liverpool Street. He said, 'You're not going to pay', and he gave us three pounds. But, of course, Cynthia had never been in a London taxi before. He opened the door of the taxi for us. I goes in, sits right down. I glanced round to see where Cynthia was. She was sitting on the floor with her legs up in the air! She didn't come far enough into the taxi before sitting down. In a London taxi, you see, the seats are set well back. I said, 'What the heck are you doing sitting down there?!' I helped her up onto the seat and we were laughing nearly all the way home. The second time we went up, I left a pair of shoes there. I bought Cynthia a pair of shoes, picked the bags up from under the seat after the meeting and I reckon I just left that one with the pair of shoes in behind. Cynthia got hot headed about it and was moaning but Mr Harvey found them and brought them down a few days later. He guessed they were ours.

One evening on our way on our bicycles to a midweek meeting in Stanstead Methodist Church she said she wanted to help the men harvest the sugar beet on Mr D. Alston's farm, Alpheton. We were still arguing when we got into the church and I struck her on the arm when we were sitting down. On the way home I flung my bicycle in the middle of the road and stamped on it. She carried on in front so I just had to get on my bike again, you know, and go home with her for supper.

I tried for a house for us on Mr Oliver's but he only had flats, a big house made into six or seven flats on somebody else's ground. We'd have had to live above somebody else and there was no garden. So I saw this job in *The East Anglian*; there's always all sorts of agricultural jobs advertised in that paper every day. Dr Norman of Brundon Hall, Sudbury, wanted a tractor driver and a relief cowman, and a house went with it.

The farm manager, Mr Vic Simmons, interviewed me and then come up to my home at Newton and told me the job was mine and my wages was eight pound a week plus five shillings an hour overtime for the relief milking. That was in February, 1960, and we managed better on that eight pound a week then than what we do on this forty pound a week now; it just don't go nowhere. The Insurance weren't a great lot and the Income Tax was ten shillings.

I took Cynthia down to the farm to see the house. She liked it. It had a front room and two bedrooms and a bathroom and a toilet and a pantry and a kitchen with a Rayburn heater, and a thirty rod garden. Then we see Dr Norman. He was in bed because he was just getting over a bad heart attack. We had a real old chat. Cynthia said, 'Do you mind us because we go out preaching and that Sundays?' He say, 'Not at all, my dear,' he say. 'I don't mind you doing that,' he say. 'My father, he was a parson and I'm a lay reader. Go ahead!'

I worked there a month and on March the 26th, 1960, Cynthia and I got married at St John's Methodist Church in Sudbury. We couldn't get married at the Mission Hall in Bridge Street because it's not licensed.

Chapter Seven

We had some wonderful times at Brundon. Dr Norman was a firm believer and lay reader in the Church of England. He would go off to church every Sunday and he'd come back and he'd very often come round and have a chat with us on the bible. He was a doctor by trade, a heart specialist. Braintree was his main hospital and he was very strict. When he went round the hospital everything had to be 'so', everything had to be spick and span. They used to be scared when he went round; the nurses say, 'Come on! All tidy today! Dr Norman's coming round today!' If I'd have had my trouble when I was down there in Sudbury he wouldn't have let me go into one of the local hospitals, he'd have took me over to his. 'In the local hospitals down here,' he say, 'you're just a body. Get over to my hospital,' he say, 'and we treat you as a patient!' When any of us was a bit dicky down on the farm there was never no need for us to go to the local doctor, he used to give you a tablet or something for it. He was very good in that way. And summertime he used to give us fruit, he always used to come round with a basket of apples. He had a wonderful orchard place with strawberries in and red currants, black currants, gooseberries. He used to come and see us and say, 'Cynthia,' —he used to call us by our Christian names—'Cynthia,' or 'Len,' he say, 'if you like you can come up to the orchard. You can pick some strawberries. You can pick some gooseberries

. . . Help yourself,' he'd say. 'Pick what you want.' When Judith used to be sitting out in the pram he used to make a real fuss of her. He said that the daughter was a real credit to us. Yes, a really wonderful man he was. Even when Judith was born and I was living at home alone like with Aunt Lizzie, my father-in-law's sister who came down to cook my meals and that, one day I met him and he say, 'Getting your meals all right, Len?' I say, 'Yes, thank you very much, Doctor.' He say, 'There's no need for you to starve, you know. You can always come up to the Hall for lunch.'

Just before we went to Brundon there was a Hungarian down there—a relief cowman and a tractor driver—and he used to knock his wife about cruel, even worse than I did. I reckon out in Hungary you've the right to do it; you can knock your wife and beat her to death if you like, they wouldn't do nothing about it. He came over to this country, you see, and he thought he could do the same. He was a terror. He used to get girls of sixteen, seventeen into trouble and wait until the baby was born and take it home to his wife and say, 'Here you are. You can bring *that* one up!' They used to go out for hours at night and leave their little girls indoors all alone. One of the neighbours went in one night and she found they'd left one of them with a bottle of aspirin to play with. He was on the cows one day and one of the chaps was driving his tractor and he went after him and started punching him on the mouth. Dr Norman say, 'It ain't your tractor,' he say, 'I employ you to drive it,' he say. 'It belongs to me,' and got rid of him.

To begin with at Norman's I was only carting muck and suchlike and doing a bit of hedging and getting the sugarbeet off the fields. Then one Wednesday I had to go into the cows in the afternoon and learn the new method of milking. I'd been used to the bucket type of milking. The new method was direct, straight to the churn. In the jobs before you used to have bucket-type machines, you used to have to put your cluster-cups onto the teats and, when your bucket was full, you used to have to take your clusters off, tip your milk out of your bucket into a pail, put the clusters back onto another cow, milk it and do the same thing again. When the pail was full someone used to cart it away and tip it so the milk went into a hopper above a cooler. The hopper held about five or six gallons and had a tap, and you turned the tap and the milk used to run down the cooler through a strainer into a ten gallon churn. When the churn was full, the chap who was carting the milk used to change it for you. The *new* way when I went to Norman's, there was pipes along above the cows, then you used to have a glass bowl come down, tubes on it and the clusters on the ends of these tubes. Then you'd have a two way tap like and you put the clusters on the cows to milk them and, when your cow was finished milking, you took the clusters off, twisted your tap the other way about and the milk was sucked up out of this bowl straight into the hopper, into the cooler, into the churn. You didn't have to cart the milk at all; all you had to do was change the churn; one of us would just nip through and change it. I did that for nearly all of the thirteen years I was down at Brundon. At first it was the relief work, Thursdays and Saturdays. Then after about eight years when one of the two cowmen retired I took his place.

I soon packed drinking up with a wife to keep but jealousy still had a hold on me and I used to knock her about if she talked to other men. Mr Rix used to grow potatoes on Clapstile Farm where we are now and she used to go over and help the men pick them up, and I used to get wild as anything.

I packed up smoking too because I got caught doing it where the milk was. Milk recorders used to come every month or so and take samples from every individual cow. Then every six months or three months or whatever inspectors took butter fat samples from the churns. They were all from the Milk Marketing Board. The milk recorders, they let you smoke. They smoked theirselves. They were just workmen.

They didn't like to make bad friends. But the butter fat inspectors, they were different and you didn't know when they were coming. One come in one day and caught us smoking and say if he caught us at it again we'd be reported to a higher official of the MMB. So I just turned it in. There's got to be three per cent butter fat in the milk. If there were no three per cent then you was in dire trouble, the inspectors wanted to find out why, what was wrong. And your cooler's got to have no copper showing or they stick a nail through it so it leaks water. One inspector, a proper brute he was. His name was Petterson. He was a Scotchman. 'That shouldn't be there!' he'd say if there was just a little bit of muck on the wall, and you'd have to take it off. *He* done something wrong one day and I caught him at it. He dipped his measure into a churn and tipped it into the bottle and he hadn't washed it from the previous farm. I dressed him down for it. A few months later I made a little mistake and he was ready. I stuck my finger in a milk churn. I said, 'You've got me now, you beggar!' and he burst out laughing! The CWS, you know, the Co-op, come every morning and took the morning's and the previous afternoon's milk in a lorry away. The inspectors could follow a lorry and stop it to take a sample. There used to sometimes be a real old tussle. The driver used to say, 'I haven't got time to wait about for you all day long! I've got to get back to the depot! Hurry up instead of talking!'

We'd been down at Brundon just over the year and somebody set fire to a big Dutch barn full of straw and hay. The doctor wasn't allowed out to see it on account of his heart condition. His wife was a-crying. A boy named —— did it. He said he liked to see the fire engine come out. He got three years for it. He was a rum kettle of fish. He'd been in trouble before, and he's still in prison now for the things he's done: he thieves as well. The whole barn was completely gutted. It was a Sunday. The wife and I had been over at the Mission Hall and we went past The White Horse pub just out through Long Melford and there was a relief fireman at the door. He say to his wife, 'I don't know what time I'll be back, dear. There's a fire at Sudbury.' My wife started to get a bit het up like in case it was our house and we got a little nearer and nearer and she say, 'Look at the glow! It looks as if it *is* down the farm,' she say, 'and the poor cats are in the house!' I say, 'It's too far back for the house.' And when we got down the drive we could see what it was, it was this big Dutch barn. There was about twelve thousand bales and that in there! The firemen were there all night. The wife and I got up and made them cups of tea. The next day we went to work and we was carting on our backs all the burnt straw to a big old sand-pit. It was still burning and we kept calling out for water. I was bent over and I shouted, 'I want some water please!' and a fireman turned his hose and soaked my backside! First we were raking it out. It was pretty dangerous because there was big cement beams all hanging loose up in the roof. We worked till nine or ten at night carting all the burnt stuff away. I'd a mechanical loader for part of the time and I was loading it onto the trailers. The fireman canteen come down with cups of tea and pork pies, and we were allowed to have a cup of tea and a pork pie whenever we wanted. 'Are we allowed?' we say, and a fireman say, 'Yes. You're one of us now!' I'd to have a bath that night. I was as black as soot. Normally I'd only have a bath on Saturdays.

When the wife and I was courting—we hadn't been going together long—there was a fire up at Mr Rix's where I'm working now. Not the main house, just the out-buildings. It was started by an electrical fault in the generating plant. Mrs Rix got up and let the bullocks out—Mr Rix was going in for pigs then, but not so big as he is now, but the fire didn't reach them. She couldn't get near enough to the calves because the heat was so intense. Then the building collapsed. I believe two were burned to death. An animal will never go away from a fire. We had a big bonfire on a field once and there was cows on there and we couldn't keep them away; they all come and stood round it. That's why they sometimes get burned. You have to be cruel to be kind to get them away; you have to beat them with a stick. After the fire the Rixes carried on as normal as possible with temporary places for the bullocks and that. They managed to save the tractors and the lorry. One range of buildings and the barn was completely gutted so they rebuilt. But they had to get the insurance and all that sorted out first.

At the time of the fire at Clapstile Farm my father-in-law was still all round general stockman. He didn't retire till 1965 when he was sixty-five, and he's seventy-six now. He was born in 1901, the same year as my father. His sister—Aunt Lizzie—became verger at Alpheton Church and he became the grave-digger, but he stopped grave-digging soon after I married Cynthia. What he used to do was he'd have to go and measure the coffin and then go down to the graveyard after work—if it was dark he'd take an old-fashioned Tilley lantern or a Tilley lamp—and measure the size of the grave with a tape-measure and peg it out to the shape of the coffin. Then he'd dig to the shape the whole way down, a foot at a time,—a 'spit' a time they used to call it—when he'd measure it. It was always right to the last inch—six foot a double grave, three foot a single. After the funeral (they like nine times out of ten to ask Mr Rix to play the organ at a funeral) he'd fill them up and make them all nice and smooth. There was a lot of comments made on them. He got one or two gifts apart from his charge because people were pleased. If people so requested he used to go down and mound them up. The family would pay the undertaker the charge for the whole funeral and the undertaker would pay him his charge for digging the grave and Aunt Lizzie for being verger. When he started he used to charge about one pound, then it went up to about two pound. I think the last one he did was five pound. When he had a stroke on May the 13th, 1972, he was writing the history of Alpheton. He was doing really well. He'd got half way. [See Appendix.]

Aunt Lizzie died on March the 4th, 1975, when she was seventy-eight. She went into the New West Suffolk with yellow jaundice. They opened her up for an 'exploratory' and the light and air woke up the cancer in her and she died of cancer on the liver. She was a wonderful old girl, she was. For the villagers of Alpheton she'd do anything. When anybody died she used to go and lay them out for a bob or two and wash them and close their eyes and tie their mouth up if there was needs to. And, Thursdays, she'd go on the bus to Sudbury to do shopping for the village. She'd get pots and pans and that, and three to four pounds' worth of fish and chips for different people—three pieces of fish with chips for one person, so many chips for another—and she never made a note. She didn't receive nothing for doing it; she was a good old girl. I used to be 'her boy, Len'. She went to Alpheton Church every Sunday morning. Some mornings she was up at five o'clock, going down on her bike to warm the church, light the fires. If the service was ten o'clock she'd go back again half past nine, help the rector get everything ready, light all the candles on the altar, give the hymn books out. She did that right up till she went into hospital at the age of seventy-seven. The church was packed right out for her funeral. They were even sitting in the choir stalls. Farmers, poor people and all sorts came round. There was anything up to fifty cars; the car park was full. My employer, Mr Rix, he played the organ. People who didn't want to give flowers, they gave donations —there was over eighty-eight pound. It went for a plaque in memory of her, you know, in the church up near the altar. She did a lot of collections for charity, you see, so she got in with the monied people like Mr and Mrs David Alston. She done the blind, Dr Barnardo's, the Red Cross; she done the Cancer Research the year Cynthia had Judith; one year she done the Deep Sea Fishermen. We had a Memorial Service in the Mission Room. Cynthia asked for donations and we raised twenty-seven pound which bought a bible and a dozen and a half new Sankey hymn books. They were dedicated by Sid Lockwood, a lay preacher and pig haulage lorry driver in Cockfield, and the Rev. Blackall, the Parish Rector of Alpheton. He was a farmer once. Then he became rector here for seven years. Then he went to Bradwell-on-Sea but he's not happy there. He was abroad for a time. He suffers from malaria.

Dr Norman went out to Africa in 1966 I think it was, when he was in his sixties. He wanted to die in harness. He went out there and within a month he was dead. Since he'd been out there that month he'd made a great influence on the Church. The churches were full Sunday by Sunday. Before he went he gave us all a present—a comb of honey each.

Mr Paul Norman, who took over, was a different kettle of fish altogether. He was mean with the fruit, unlike his father. But at Christmastime he give us five pound and occasionally he'd give us a wood-pigeon or a duck or a pheasant. And if you wanted time off he was good that way, and in the mornings the children of the workers didn't have to walk to school if it was wet, he used to take them to all their different schools in his car. He wasn't as nice as his father but he was very good in many ways. He wouldn't have done anything like Mr Rix, building a bungalow in our garden or anything like that. The garden belonged to this cottage and he's taken it to build a bungalow for his son Peter who's getting married next year. The Ministry of Agriculture wouldn't let him take any agricultural land from the farm so he couldn't build the bungalow anywhere else. Last year in the autumn he told us all about it and we couldn't say nothing. The forestry worker that's attached to us, he's lost his half-share of it as well. We're left with only enough to keep our pets and hens and a little bit more. We used to have peas, cabbages, potatoes. Now it's only just big enough to grow potatoes on.

Clapstile Cottage has two bedrooms, front-room, bathroom, toilet and kitchen, but we ain't got a big enough pantry for Cynthia—Cynthia's a hoarder like her mother. There's tins of fruit at the bottom of the stairs—honestly speaking, she's got enough stuff in this house to set up a shop, we could last out six months, I should reckon! I reckon she's got a nearly half hundredweight of tea and ten gallons of soft drinks and these tins and tins of fruit and baked beans and soups and I should reckon about half a hundredweight of sugar. I used to tell her about it and she used to say, 'You never know! You never know when you'll be ill and can't work and need the money!' That's what she does it for—and because the prices keep going up. And we ain't got so much up here now as what we had down at Brundon. At Brundon we had more pantry room. One time when they modernised the houses we had to go into the next house while they done ours out. The builders were having a laugh as we moved our stuff. There was twenty-two cartons of pepper, about twenty bottles of vinegar . . . Later we was flooded out. The waters came up about two or three inches and I was throwing tins on the settee out of the way of the water.

In about 1970 Mr Norman sold the cows right out because the relief blokes weren't reliable. They was supposed to come at five o'clock in the morning and there'd be some of them would turn up at nine o'clock when the work was finished. He got fed up with it. So I went onto the pigs. I liked that. I don't mind what animal it is as long as it ain't sheep. I don't like sheep at all, I detest them. I don't like the smell; they've a horrible smell. They say pigs have but you can keep them clean. I wouldn't work with sheep for a thousand pound a week. That's one job I would never do: sheep. Give me anything to do with other animals and it don't worry me. I'd do anything with horses, bullocks, cows and pigs, but sheep, no fear!

I was sort of relief pigman. The pigman's name was Stan Bird. I went in at seven o'clock. He said, 'Give this lot two pailfuls, this lot half a pailful . . . This type of meal here is for the rearing. This type of meal here is for the fattening. And that lot over that corner is for the sows.' There was barley meal, maize, and fishmeal which was a concentrate all mixed up. We used to grind the barley and then you had a mixer to mix the other stuff in with it. You'd give a sow about 3½lb. per feed and the weaners would have about 4lb. per feed and the piglets would have Creep pellets—they're little tiny nuts with apple in them to make them tasty with vitamins A, B and C and so much copper. You don't weigh the pellets off at all, you just give the piglets as much as they'll eat. Your machinery's set to time and when everything's mixed up you bag it off and you take the different mixes where you want them for the week's feeding. You did one week's mixing at a time. Here at Clapstile I do it four or five times a week. The system at Norman's was a different sort of concentrate; the machinery was much the same. A year or so before I left, he went over from dry feeding to wet feeding. He had a pipeline put up so we didn't have to cart the food round by hand. Mr Rix is going to have a *dry* pipeline up here. He's got dry pipeline feeding in the weaning shed already.

The fatteners are being brought up to go to slaughter. Mr Norman's pigs would take about twenty to thirty weeks; he'd send them at about 129 to 130 pounds. It turned to kilogrammes while I was with Mr Rix. It don't worry me to see them going to be slaughtered, no. There's always more coming along. It says in the Bible, in Deuteronomy, that God provided certain meats that we should eat and shouldn't eat. According to the Old Testament we shouldn't eat pigs by rights, but in the New Testament that's all been changed. I wouldn't eat my home animals, the rabbits and that. But you must have a certain amount of meat; it's good for the blood. When my father-in-law was very ill and had very low blood pressure, the doctors demanded that he must have plenty of meat, especially liver.

At Norman's we had thirty to forty pigs and about two hundred little pigs. You'd feed them, clean them out and, when you'd finished, you'd go on the land till you started feeding them again at about four o'clock in the afternoon. When Stan had a week-off I used to do everything myself. For Mr Rix here I do almost everything myself most of the time.

I love animals as much as I do God—they're all to do with Him. As a matter of fact I may be up late tonight [4th August, 1977]. A sow's farrowing. You can tell they're farrowing because they've got milk. You feel under them and if they've got the milk they'll be farrowing in an hour or two's time. If you don't go, you can go in the next morning and you'll see about six or seven piglets dead. You see, when they're born some of them come out with a skin over their mouth and they can't breathe and you have to stick your finger in the mouth, open it like. It isn't very often it happens but there is that risk. Otherwise they just go under an infra-red light and you can leave them.

The sows usually farrow themselves. You leave them two hours but, if they're breathing heavily and straining, you know then there's one hung up. You go over to the house, ask for a pail of warm water and some Dettol, and get behind the sow and roll up your sleeve as far as you can get it and soak the arm well so it will slide easy. Then you put your hand right inside and feel to see if there's one hung up and you get hold of a leg or anything and draw it out slowly and she's all right then. Some come backwards—they should come forwards but with a sow it don't make no difference. The Dettol protects both of you: if there's anything wrong with your arm or anything wrong with the sow you're protected both ways. And when they're born and dried up you lay the little pigs squealing across your legs and you snip the teeth off with a pair of clippers because if they bite the sow when they're suckling she won't let them have the milk. You just snip the points off—two on the top, two on the bottom. Then after three days you have to give the piglets an iron injection in the ham muscle on the hind leg—two c.c.s per pig. You stick your hypodermic into a bottle just like a doctor, pick the piglet up, pull the skin tight in the ham muscle and away you go. If the sows are ill I've to inject them too. The first injections I ever done were up here at Mr Rix's. I watched it done at Mr Norman's; I do it here alone. Sometimes you get deformed piglets. I'd one down there a few months back; it'd got two heads. They've got to be destroyed. You just hit them on the head with a hammer and throw them on the muck hill to go on the fields and rot down. Some have five legs, some only have two and some have three and some have legs the wrong way up like wings. It's because they're too closely bred, the father serving his daughters like, you know. We have to change the boars every so often when we're keeping the boars' daughters for sows.

We've forty sows. Say you take the sow away from her piglets to wean her on a Thursday afternoon—Friday, Saturday, Sunday and she'll be ready to serve again Monday or Tuesday. The sow don't worry when her litter's taken away from her as much as what a cow will. A cow will keep roaring and bellowing for a calf for two or three days sometimes; sometimes she'll break out of the meadow to see it.

You must never let two boars get together: they'll fight to the death. I've got one boar up one end and one boar down the other end. I serve a sow, say, with Charlie in the morning and serve her with Archie in the afternoon. If you can serve a sow two to three times with two boars serving you get more pigs, you can get sixteen, seventeen, eighteen pig a litter. If there's a pig on store, you feed her first. Get No. 56 out—all the sows have got numbers—, take her down to the boar, let the boar out and stand there while the boar serves. Then when he's finished put them back again. He'll serve two or three in a day. You plan it all out, you write it all down. You put down when the sow is served, then you've got to work out a three-week date in case she comes on store again, and if she don't come out in three weeks you've got to have a six-week date. You know when a sow's on store and waiting to be served because other sows keep jumping on her back or else she swells up behind. Then you put down your farrowing date. Farrowing takes four months from being served. When they get near to farrowing they bag up, but your dates are down. I've got one to farrow on the 5th [August] and two on the 6th, another one on the 19th and two on the 25th—you can guarantee the dates within three or four days. Then you leave the sow on the little pigs for five weeks, take her off on the five weeks' date, shove her back in the sow barn and in five or six days she'll be ready for serving again.

The two boars I've got are all right, but some boars can be vicious with a human. You can never trust them. They could rip you to pieces with their tusks. These two are quiet enough. I sit on their back and rub their heads. But you've got to be careful, you've got to keep your eye on them the whole time. You can't stand right in front of them and just keep walking! A boar cost about £200. It's always better to buy another boar instead of a sow. If you buy sows you start buying in trouble—disease and that. Some people got a lot in round here a few weeks back and they've got nothing but trouble. They couldn't get them in pig or nothing.

You can do artificial insemination with sows but it's an expensive game. With the cows, though, at Norman's before Mr Norman sold out we never had a bull—it was all by artificial insemination. Each service was one pound five shillings. Men used to have to come out from Colchester. They'd have the semen in little bottles kept in nitrogen, a big round tank of bottles with all different semens of different bulls. They'd just file the top off, draw the semen into a glass tube, stick it up the cow and press the end, you know, with one hand while they'd the other up the back passage to feel for the womb. The bottles kept for months and months, years, in that stuff, the nitrogen. You mustn't put your hand in it: it'll burn it off nearly.

At Mr Norman's I helped to give the cows a drench to clear them out; you poured a bottle of liquid down their throat. And I used to have to stick them for the wind—that's ramming a long knife in a round steel sheath into the hollow of their side. You draw the knife out, leaving the sheath in, and all the wind comes out. Phhhhh—you'd want a gas-mask on! Then you pull the sheath out and the skin heals. When they've got milk fever you've got to get the vet out. He sticks a needle in a vein in the back and lets a bottle of magnesium stuff run in and the cow's walking about within ten minutes. When they've milk fever it's from having too much milk and not enough calcium when they calve. They can't stand up, they fall over, and if you don't treat them they die.

The first bit of surgery I ever had to do with pigs was castrating them. I done it a month at Norman's before I came up here. Someone holds the boar pig upside down for you between his legs while you operate. You make an incision in between the back legs with a knife, nip out the testicles, cut away the skin, cut the cords off and throw the lot away to the sows who eat them. You must do them, if possible, at three weeks old. If you do them at five weeks, say, they don't do so well, it pulls them down in growth. They reckon if you don't castrate the bacon's got a stronger taste to it which people don't like. Some of the boars scream if you nip them too tight. I've done over a hundred in an hour. They're trying to give it out now that you must put them to sleep like you've to do with tom-cats.

When the pigs have abscesses come on the neck, on the bag, on the leg, after fighting and biting, I cut them open and let the stuff out. Peter was with me once. I asked for some warm water so that I could bathe an abscess first and he say, 'Can I come and have a look?' So I got the knife and slit it and nipped it and all the stuff come out, and when I looked round for Peter he weren't there no more, he'd disappeared. It's all horrible stuff, white pus, that comes out, you know. Then the Governor come—'Ugh! How can you do it!' I say, 'Go on! Go on! Cheerio!' Same as if anybody's sick in the house—*I* have to clear it all up. The wife can't do it. I'd even to clean up Judith when she was a baby. Nothing worries me.

I left Mr Norman in 1973 because I don't believe in harvesting on a Sunday. I'd work for cattle, pigs or anything like that; they need feeding, you can't leave them. But land work, that can be left. He was getting a bit short of cash and he sold his pigs out and there wasn't enough work for all of us to do. He didn't give me the sack. When his father died he became a lay reader as well—he can give sermons in any Church of England church; he's been over to Alpheton. No, we heard it wasn't his fault, it was one of the other workers complaining being that we went to church. This present employer, he won't give me harvesting on a Sunday. He's a methodist and he preaches round about on the Methodist circuit—Bury, Leavenheath, Sudbury, Stanstead, Glemsford . . . There's so many churches to a circuit.

I saw the job—pigman and tractor driver—advertised in *The Suffolk Free Press.* It's called *The Suffolk Free Press* because certain things you can put in free, like letters. Mr Norman gave us a month's notice and if I hadn't got a job within a month he wouldn't have turned us out; he was too kind hearted to do that. This employer phoned up to him for references and that to see if I was right or not and he say, 'Now,' he says, 'look here, Mr Rix!' he says. 'I like Len and I want you to look after him! If you're not going to look after him I shan't let him go!' When I was ill and that with cancer he was always making inquiries about me. I met him in Sudbury one day and we was talking and he said to me, 'It's so nice to see you, Len. You've had a pretty rough time, haven't you?' I said, 'How did you know?' He said, 'Oh, we've been making inquiries all about you.'

So I got this new job as pigman and tractor driver with Mr Rix at Clapstile Farm, Alpheton, just after harvest in September, 1973. By the time I left Mr Norman I was earning about £22 to £24 take home pay a week. Money went so much further then. For the money you'd pay for a joint of meat now you'd get a huge joint then.

Before overtime my weekly wage now is about £40.50 and my take home about £36.71. There's no rent to pay because the cottage—Clapstile Cottage—is 'tied'. I get more than what the general farm-worker do—two to three pound more a week. It's the responsibility, you see, seeing as I've got to attend the pigs. The Transport and General Workers Union have put in for some more money but I don't belong to it. I don't want to cause no upsets or anything with anybody but I think what's ruining the country is the unions. They keep asking for more money and less hours' work and there ain't so much productivity. I read in *The East Anglian* the other day that they want sixty pound a week for a thirty-five hour week. I do forty hours basic and I've to look after stock. They're asking too much. I mean, there won't be so much work done and it'll cost the farmer more for overtime for the harvest work and that. It's unfair to the farmer. It's the tax that's spoiling everything. The more money people get the more tax they've got to pay. I do three hours' overtime for just over a pound an hour. But you lose nearly all your overtime in tax; you're working for nothing. Say you was to work fourteen hours overtime at harvest you wouldn't bring half of it home.

This country's getting in such a terrible state. Everybody wants to do less work for more money. And I reckon there's far too many coming into this country from overseas to take the work up from *us*. I've got a relation and he won't give to collections like Christian Aid for the starving and that, he say, 'Why don't they put in the work that we have to?!' Out in these foreign countries the women work and the men sort of laze about all day long. I reckon the men should be made to work in the countries where they belong and then there wouldn't be these starving millions. I believe that people today,—I can bring religion in?—I believe that people today are falling away from God. That's why this country of ours is in such a state—there's so much greed and so little hard work. It's up to us who 'believe' to tell them about Jesus.

Chapter Eight

The following prayer and message were spoken by Mrs Mills during evening worship at the Free Church Mission Room, Bridge Street, Suffolk, on Sunday, 21st August, 1977:—

O God who is our Father, once again we draw before You in prayer. We would ask that You will bless these gifts which have been given by these Thy children. We would ask that You will take them, Lord, and use them for the furtherance of Thy work in here, this little wayside Bethel. And our main desire tonight, Lord, is to see these chairs full and not empty. We would ask You to answer our prayers and send the people from these two villages around us to fill these chairs that we may see not even one empty. We would ask that they may come in needing Thy Word and going out with Thy Word implanted upon their hearts. And now Lord as we meditate upon Your Word we would ask that You will be with Your servant who will be Your mouthpiece. We ask this in Jesus' precious name. Amen.

For our message tonight we're going to look for just a little while at the chapter that we read together—St Luke's Gospel, Chapter Fourteen. We're going to look mainly at the latter part of it, beginning with the man who made a supper. As you know, it's a very well known story, one very often read and spoken upon in God's house. It doesn't give us the name of the man, it just says a certain man made a great supper and he bade many. And this man, we don't know what he prepared but probably it was something that was very nice and good to taste, but he wanted to enjoy his supper with other people. He had made this great meal and he wanted people to come in and to share it with him. You know the story, don't you? They all with one accord began to make an excuse. And it records three excuses here in God's Word. The first one said unto Him, 'I have bought a piece of ground,' and he wanted to go and see it, which meant, I suppose, that he wanted to go and see if it was in the condition that he needed, if it was the right sort of piece of ground that he wanted and to see if it was big enough to suit his needs. And then the next one said, 'I've bought five yoke of oxen and I must go to prove them.' And so he couldn't come either. He wanted to go and view the stock that he had bought to take to his farm. And then the third one, he made another excuse and he said, 'I have married a wife and I can't come.' That may perhaps be a genuine excuse, but I feel like this, that when you get married you shouldn't make excuses for either one side or the other, you should go into God's house together or these two should have gone to this supper that this man had made together. But rather than the two go, the one said he would stay away, he would put his wife before a meal, perhaps the right thing to do and the wrong way to go about it. But when we get further into the story you will see what I mean. But when the three excuses had been made the servant came and showed this Lord these things. And the master of the house naturally was angry because he had made this supper and he wasn't at all pleased because he wanted the things eaten. And he said to the servant, 'Well you must go out quickly into the streets, you must bring in other people. Will you go out now, please, and bring in the poor and the maimed and the halt and the blind?' This man was determined to help someone and so he decided to help the ones that were incapacitated. And the servant said, 'Lord, it is done as thou hast commanded', and yet there was room. You see this man must have had a big hall to get all these people in and have still room for any more because he said, 'I want you now to go out into the highways and the hedges and compel them to come in that my house may be full.' And he also said, 'I say unto you, that none of those men which were bidden shall taste of my supper.' And so we're not told much more about this story, we are just told the story that they were bidden to come to the feast. But today we can look on another side of this story, can't we? God Himself in heaven has made a great feast. He's making this feast every day. And He's making this for His children who will love Him and serve Him every day of their lives. Jesus said, 'Come unto Me. I need you. I want you to come out of your sin, out of your shame, out of the mire and clay of the ground and come into My house. I want you to serve Me.' But there are so many around us today who will not even think of coming into His house, let alone listen to His words. Tonight I suppose that in this church, owing to the weather, there will be about five or six listening to the Word of God. You see people today do not want the Word of God in their hearts. When we used to go to chapel when we were small, when we used to go to Sunday School, at least we knew that in God's house on a Sunday afternoon there would be twenty children. In those days people were more ready for the Word than they are today. As you can see here tonight, you are four in the congregation. Yet God says, 'I rejoice because you have kept my door open. The door is open that people may come in to My feast. That is My will.' And that is the kind of feast that God wants us to enjoy. There are many people tonight around outside living across the road who could come in and listen to the Word of God. What is the supper or the feast that God has prepared for us? It is His will that we gather here tonight in His house and He is speaking to men, women and children alike. He wants them. He wants you. He wants me. He wants us all to be His children. Are we going to make excuses like these three people here did in His words in St Luke's Gospel? Are we going to make some excuse for not going to a place of worship? I can remember the time when *I* made a few excuses, and the rest of the day didn't go right, because God had bidden me to go into His House and that's where I should have been, and yet I made excuses to be away from the House of God. And that is the trouble with the world around us today. Too many people are not prepared to go into the House of God. They are not prepared to listen. They won't even have his Book in their house and read it. Some years ago I knew someone who had put a bible in a sale in their yard at Alpheton—it used to be the village Public House. And as my father went down to this sale, he set his eyes upon this bible, it was a huge family bible and he asked the price of it and they said he could have it for a shilling because no one wanted it. And before he could pick it up someone kicked it right across the sale-room and said, 'We don't want that sort of thing in our house. It's nothing, only fairy tales.' But anyhow my father got it and he brought it home and he gave it to me and, as far as I know, I've still got it at home somewhere. It's all in pieces but it doesn't matter, it's still God's Word. You see, my friends tonight, that's what people think of God and His Word today. All they want to do is to kick it out of the way. They want to curse His name and to scorn and mock Him the same as they did when He was crucified upon the cross. And so they make all kinds of excuses to get out of the way. You see, the servant said that he had done *all* that was commanded. But is there no more that *we* can do? Have we done all that God has commanded in our lifetime? I wouldn't like to say we have. Have we been out into the highways and the hedges and have we asked them to come in that God's house may be filled? We may have been to a few doors in our time and asked them and, when we had the scorning finger, we may have been afraid to go out again. And yet we know that there are many people even round this little place tonight who could do with the Word of God in their hearts. We think of only the other day when we were told that one of our great pop singers [Elvis Presley] had died in America. When they put his body on view for the public to file past—and I don't know how many thousands there were that went past—some of them, it's said, when they came out said that he looked ill and that he didn't look like the person they went in to see. And they were shedding tears of grief because their pop idol had died. I wonder if Jesus was down here today and He were, like we say, an ordinary human being, I wonder, if He died, whether people would run in to view His body, whether they would come out and say, 'It doesn't look like Jesus,' or whether they would be the other way round. I think it more likely they would be scorning and mocking Jesus because in this world today He is not needed according to the world at large. Yet you and I need Him. We need Him every day and minute of our lives. You've heard this story before—Dad has told it down here—of a man who one year sowed a field of beans—it was in this village—and they began to come up thick and a good crop of beans began to grow. And another man came one day and went into the field with this farmer and he said to him, 'You've got a beautiful field of beans there!' He said, 'Yes, I have, haven't I? And they'll be all right if God leaves them alone. If God keeps his hands off them, I'll have a good crop to harvest.' And, believe it or not, God did leave that field alone, and that man didn't harvest one pod of beans off that field, they just withered away and died right down to the ground. He didn't want God, he didn't want God to help him. And so God left everything alone. And, you see, it so is in the world today. People don't want God. They put Him on one side, they cast Him out of their lives, and they say today, 'Away with Him! Crucify Him! *We* don't want this man to rule our lives. We want to run our own lives. We want to go our own way.' What are *we* going to do tonight? Are *we* going the right way on the path of life towards God? Or are we on the downward path that leads to a lost eternity? Tonight, my friends, I challenge you. If you don't know God in the full meaning of what it is, I ask you before it is too late to come down on your knees and pray that God will forgive you, that God will take you into His fold that means that you will attain everlasting life. Most of us anyway, I trust that all of us do, we know what it is to have God in our hearts. In a time of need, in a time of trouble, in a time of anxiety, we know what it is to call upon God and to ask Him to come into our lives again, afresh, and help us through these troubles. And many is the time that I myself can say that God has helped. He has taken us through many times of trouble and temptation and illness. When Judith was a baby, for three weeks it was touch and go. And yet God heard our humble prayers and He gave Judith back to us again. You see, people today won't believe that God can heal. We know that God can do these things because He's done it so many times for our family that we've got to know that God is a real friendly, wonderful Father to each one of us. But you see, these people here, they are *away* from God, and that is the trouble with the world now. They want to live their own lives. They want to make a career of their lives. But they don't want God to help them and to be in it. In verse thirty-three we are told, 'So likewise, whosoever he be of you that forsaketh not all that he hath, he cannot be My disciple' Are we Jesus' disciples tonight? If we are, then we should go out in His work and in His words and do His work. We should go out and proclaim the wonderful Word of God that we sang about in our second hymn, and we should not be ashamed to own God as our Saviour because we know that Jesus really lives tonight, we know He is with us and we know He will be with us till the end of our time. It says here that salt is good, but if the salt hath lost its savour, wherewith shall it be salted. You see, if we have loved the Lord and yet our love gets faded in past years, that is the same sort of meaning. We have lost our love for God and we've got to rekindle it, we've got to ask God to come afresh into our lives to rekindle that flame in our hearts. There used to be several people in this village who used to come into our little wayside Bethel, Sunday nights by Sunday nights, and tonight they are still alive but they have no desire to come into God's house, the flame has got so low that it has at last gone out. What are *we* going to do with Jesus, then? Are we going to let Him continue in our lives? Are we going to continue to love Him? Or are we going to cast Him out onto one side? I trust tonight that, as God has helped us in the past, we shall be able to say, 'Lord, You stay in my heart, in *our* hearts and in our lives, that we may be still Your servants and go out wheresoever You shall call us. Because each day of our lives God has something fresh to give us to do. God has a calling, He has a work. And for those of us that have served Him for many, many years, we trust tonight that He will continue to help us, and we shall help Him by proclaiming His gospel to the needy, to the sick, to the aged and to those that can't get out. At the little place now where I work, God is badly needed. It's only a few hours a week but there are two dear little children, one of nine months and one of three years, and Mummy has gone off and left them and left Daddy behind as well. And it's hard to see them when they cry and they call, 'Mummy!' And the other day—it really went home to my heart—the little boy found a small photo, only about two inches square, and he came to me and he put his arms around my neck and he cried, 'This is my Mummy!' You see, those little ones need loving. But Jesus loves them but, you see, there's no one there to tell them of Jesus. And in my own way I try to tell them that there *is* someone who loves them. But, you see, they say, 'Well, where *is* Jesus? We can't see Him.' And when they are so tiny and so young, it's a job to tell them of the love of Jesus. We can give them love. I try in my own sweet way to give the little ones love because they need it. But, you see, they need Mother. They need a friend.

But they need Jesus also, they need Jesus in the home. I'd like to ask you tonight to pray for that home because it badly needs Jesus, all of them do. Well, I wonder tonight if we are loving people as we should love them. Is there not someone around here that we can go and visit and try to put a word in their ears from God's words? Is there not someone who we can give a friendly smile to or a kindly word, a word of comfort, a word of cheer, and tell them that in this world, although they may live alone, God is with them and He loves them? Let us not, then, be as some people, and leave God out of everything and out of our lives! It may be tomorrow that God will call one of us into His presence. We know not. This may be our last Sunday night here. I don't mean to spread fear and guilt but we never know when God may come back to take us to Himself. Have we done the work and the task that God has set us to do? Have we done all that He has given us to do in His service? I have known Jesus since the age of eleven, and I've never known Him to let me down once, either at school or at work or in my time at home. I've never known Jesus to be away. He's always been beside me. He's been my chief guide and guardian and protector. And, when Len was away, God was with me; I wasn't alone. Sometimes we may have had little fears in our hearts, but God came back and said, 'Fear not, for I am with you.' So then, let us keep Jesus in our hearts, let us not make vain excuses for not coming to His House. Let us keep Him in our hearts, shut the door of our hearts and lock it fast that God may live and grow there for evermore. Amen.

Chapter Nine

I work eight till five week-days, with an hour off for dinner and Saturdays and Sundays eight till nine thirty.

I get up six to half past, put the kettle on for the tea, then make the tea, have a cup myself, then pour the wife one—she gets up about the same time—and bring Judith one with a bun and her cat, Sooty. Her cat always calls out as soon as I get my own cup out of the pot! She'll call and call until I bring her up. Well, I don't actually bring her up, I leave her to the foot of the stairs and I say, 'Go on! Go on and call her!' and she'll go to her door and she'll call out to her, 'Miaow! Miaow-aow!', she'll keep till she gets up and opens the door and lets us in.

Altogether we've got twelve cats—Sooty, Twinkle, Topsy, Smut, Ginger, Smoky or Little Miss Big Eyes, Tabby, Pluppy, Pandy, Woolly, Star and Sparky. Then we've got a dog, a labrador crossed boxer called Gipsy; three game banties: Annabel, Diane and Diana; five hens, two cockerels and five ordinary banties; one budgie: Sammy; two hamsters: Scrooge and Sherry; and eleven rabbits—Bambi, Bimbo, Spotty, Squeak, Sweep, George, Puffin and Muffin, Soot, and Dimple and Dapple. They're all fed twice a day except for the cats, the dog and the budgie and the hamsters; the cats and the dog are fed three times a day, and the budgie and hamsters once. The wife does it in the mornings unless she's going out anywhere, then I help her. I feed the rabbits at night and if she's terribly busy Judith or myself will feed the cats. She and Judith take Gipsy for walks. The hens and banties and the cockerels have wet layers' mash and bread in the morning, all mixed in, and in the afternoon they have wheat or a mixture of wheat, flake-maize and oats. The hamsters have 'hamster food' with sunflower seeds in and monkey nuts and bits of broken biscuit and wheat, barley and oats. The budgie has Trill. The cats in the morning, they'll have paste on bread all cut up for them—eight rounds, sometimes ten; then for lunch they'll have Crunchies or Munchies or Capital F; at night then they'll have bread and paste or a tin of Felix or Kit-e-kat with bread in. More often than not they'll prefer water to milk. Mornings and lunchtime they have water. At night they'll have milk as well. The dog will have bread and paste in the morning and at dinnertime he'll have his Bonios or dogbiscuits; at night he'll have paste and bread or, if the cats have a tin of meat, he'll share that. In the mornings the rabbits'll have bread; at night any green stuff that's available—cow mumble, sheep's parsley, dandelion leaves, bellboyne, cabbage leaves, lettuce leaves, sugar beet leaves . . . but *they* wants really to lay a day or two to get the acid out or it'll make them scour, they'll get the trots.

I like the cats the best. They're so affectionate, I reckon. The little black and white cat is mine—Woolly—and the three game banties. We don't let the cats out in case they run onto the road. They've a dirt box in the kitchen.

Seven o'clock I have my breakfast—bacon or a pork pie or a Cornish pasty (one morning I had a yoghourt instead), another cup of tea and bread and marmalade or jam, then a few cakes. I'm a terror for cakes first thing in the morning—fruit buns or scones or mince pies or sausage rolls. The wife and Judith have their breakfast later or, when Judith is going to school, she has it with me before the bus collects her at ten past eight. Judith likes to have bacon and egg and beans and a fried slice.

Five to eight, off to work I go, get to the farm, go round all the pigs first to see if there's any missing or not. You have to check your numbers every day because sometimes there's rustlers around, you know, that steal the pigs and go off with them. You see, too, if there's any illnesses and if there is,—the quicker you do it the better—you just have to get the hypodermic out and give injections—chloramphenicol, Trivetrin, Ilcocillin, sulphamethazine, Orojet, Leodex, Jectadine . . . usually in the ham muscle or the neck. The Ilcocillin's for mastitis or a discharge—6 c.c.'s. The Orojet is for enteritis or scours—there's a tube attached to the bottle and I put that into the pig's mouth and give two squirts. The sulphamethazine that's for when they go thin very suddenly and scour very bad. You turn the pig right upside down and give it 5 c.c.'s right in the gut and within an hour or two it's improving. Leodex is for the piglets when they're three days old to stop them getting anaemia. Jectadine's for the sows to build them up a bit before going to the boar. You need pituitary for slow pigging. You leave them two hours and after two hours if they keep heaving and straining and haven't any more pigs you give them an injection of 1 c.c. in the neck and that will help them. You must not give them more than 1 c.c. You give them more than one and that will close the womb right up and they won't have any more pigs. You also use pituitary to let the milk down—2 c.c. pituatary with 6 c.c. of Ilcocillin mixed together. For worms you give Nilverm just under the skin behind the ear. You've got to be very careful you don't stick the needle in the jugular vein or the pig will die. You can tell when a pig has worms because it's thin and the tail is not curled, it hangs straight down.

Sometimes we have to call the vet out if a sow's gone wrong inside like and you daren't do it yourself. Sometimes we'll have a sow rick its back and you don't quite know how to treat it and he'll have to come to see it, you know, just give it an injection of antibiotics. We had some gilts once—they wouldn't come on store—so we had the vet out to give them a deep intra-muscular injection. We try to do all we can ourself because to get the vet out, I mean, just for the journey, it costs six pound. From Hadleigh, that's six pound—just to come from Hadleigh to the farm before he do anything! There's six of them, you know, work together. At night there's always one on call so you ring the depot like—the place where they have the surgery—and there'll be a self-answering telephone and it'll say, 'This is the veterinary surgeons Lemon and Sutherland. Mr Paul Ryde is on call. Telephone Bildeston 212.'—or something like that. Mr Lemon has retired. Sutherland, you know, is the head one now. I've had students come up to the farm, you know, learning the veterinary side. There was one girl that come round with Mr Sutherland just a few weeks back; she was from Sweden. One or two pigs had died and he cut them open, you know, to see what it was and it was bowel oedema—that's something that goes wrong with the bowels and the pig blows up with poisoning and dies.

If a pig don't get no water it gets salt poisoning. They go mad then: they go funny in the head. Sometimes you have to be out and the drinker will get blocked up with rust and that and there's no water coming through. That's when you get into trouble. You can save them sometimes if you're quick enough, you know, get a pail in there and cop some pails of water in and they'll drink it up. But sometimes you're too late, they just die of salt poisoning, toxaemia. My wife had it when Judith was born. She'd too much salt in the body and it was touch and go for them both.

If your food's already in the barrows—they're big three-wheel galvanised tin barrows holding 5 to 6 cwt.—you feed the sows in the farrowing shed first and give the little pigs their creep pellets. There are fourteen sows, some with sixteen piglets. Then I go to the sow barn to the rest of the sows.

Them and the boars have their meal the same, then I go over to the fattening shed to feed the seventy or eighty porkers. Then there's about a hundred weaners in the weaning shed to be fed as well. Then I take the mix off the hopper and fill up the barrows ready for the afternoon and the next day if they're running low. Your barley comes from a bin, goes up the auger—a big pipe with a spiral that twizzles round inside worked by an electric motor—and into the hopper. The rest of the mix—the concentrate and that—goes into the hopper by hand, and I switch on the mixer and it all mixes up. The machinery's set to time. Say you want 5 cwt. of barley, you set your clock to 5 and when you've got your 5 cwt. of barley the machine switches off—5, 4, 3, 2, 1, zero, it switches off. I put the barley in the mill hopper and one of Mr Rix's sons turns it on for me at night because it's cheaper. Summertime it's seven o'clock and wintertime it's eight o'clock, the cheap rate. For the fatteners and the weaners there's different mixes of barley and Growercorn. The sows get so much barley, 'middlings' (that's a by-product of milling wheat) and concentrate—that's a special protein mix of fishmeal, iron and copper, and that stuff you must not let sheep or any other animal have access to because the copper would kill them.

When I've fed the pigs I don't hear nothing of them all day. Only when I go to feed them again and they know I'm coming they'll start to squeal. It's funny about animals. Other people go past their doors and that at feeding times and they don't take no notice. But when they hear *me*—whether they hear the sound or get the scent or what—they all start to squeal!

Mucking out is on Mondays and Fridays. If there's a Bank Holiday or anything like that on a Monday it's done on a Tuesday. Open all the main gates—you know, each pen has got a gate to it—, clean out any muck inside the sleeping quarters (sometimes they'll muck inside but not very often), reverse the tractor with the scraper on the back into what we call the dunging passage, scrape all the muck down to the muck dungle and do that, carry on, you know, that procedure about half a dozen times till your finished. Then, once a week, you go to the Dutch barn and get your bales of straw and take two to each of the sleeping quarters because when the straw gets short and dusty the pigs start to sneeze. They spread it about theirselves. Sometimes the little pigs will dung inside their sleeping quarters and you've to throw the muck into the passage with a fork. For the pigs coming up for slaughter it's a different procedure. You've got sliding doors so the pigs can't get into the dunging passage. So you have to have two tractors. You have one tractor on the trailer and you have another tractor that's got a fork-lift on, and you dung out, drive your tractor in, get a forkful, reverse out, forward again, tip it onto the trailer, and when you've got a trailer load you drive off round to your muck dungle, tip your trailer up, come back, do the same procedure again, sometimes four times, sometimes six. That's only got to be done about once a month. The new tractors we've got now have got the safety cabs but we had to put roll-bars on the old ones. We call them roll-bars because if the tractors roll over they save you getting killed or seriously injured. We got a roll-bar put on the tractor what's got the hydraulic fork-lift for cleaning out the dunging passages. The top half will fold back so you can get into the low buildings but as soon as you've done that job in the low building, that bar must come back over the top again and the pins put through because, if you use a tractor without the safety-frame or cab on, you're liable to a fifty pound fine. Not only the employer gets fined but I get fined as well: I can get fined for using it without it on and he can get fined for not having it on. But he, hisself, Mr Rix, can drive a tractor without it on: he don't need a guard or nothing—that's if he don't employ nobody else on the farm.

I sing most of the time I'm working, even when I'm feeding the pigs. The boss comes in sometimes and he'll say, 'Are you happy?' or something like that, you know. Sometimes I'll sing choruses

Turn your eyes upon Jesus
Look full in His wonderful face
And the things of earth will grow strangely dim
In the light of His glory and grace

—that comes from one of the CCSM books of choruses. There's five books of them, One, Two, Three, Four and Five, including children's choruses—'I Will Make You Fishers Of Men', 'Jesus Wants You For A Sunbeam', 'We Are Building Day By Day' . . . I sing those and all; they're helpful.

What a friend we have in Jesus,
All our sins and griefs to bear!
What a privilege to carry
Everything to God in prayer!

—that's a hymn. And I sing 'Oh for a closer walk with God . . .'— I don't know that one too well. Then there's 'Amazing Grace':

Amazing grace! how sweet the sound
That saved a wretch like me;
I once was lost but now am found
Was blind, but now I see.

Peter, the youngest son, was asking me how I was getting on with the book and all that, and I say there was a record going with it, perhaps, and I say, 'You'll buy the record, won't you?' He say, 'No fear! I get enough of your voice all day long!' He was twenty-one last year. He's the one who's getting married next year, the one who's having the bungalow built. I should reckon Trevor is about twenty-five, twenty-six. If Mr Rix is away, Trevor, he's the boss, he takes over. He ain't got no young ladies—he makes too many faces. You can't help laughing. I don't think he realises what he's doing. He sits there on the tractor sometimes, you know, and once we were putting the beet harvester in the tractor shed, you see, because it was raining, and the youngest one, Peter, was directing Trevor in and I was with them and Trevor was pulling faces and Peter said, 'What are you doing that for?' and looked at me and pulled a face hisself and I didn't know where to look for laughing! Peter was taking the mickey out of him, you see. Peter likes a laugh; he's a comical boy. A pig knocked him over the other day and I stood there roaring with laughing and he come and grabbed a hold of me and laid me on the ground as well. Oh we do have a bit of fun together.

I had a boar out, Archie, one Wednesday morning. I took him round to a sow and used him, and I was just going to take him back and Judy started coming round the corner and all at once he took to his heels and runned and Judy runned as well! I'd to go in front of him and turn him. You must keep an eye on them though you don't have to have them on a lead. Just before I came here, when I was at Norman's, Harry Green, a nasty bad-tempered chap, had a boar and it wouldn't go through where he wanted it to and he struck on to it and it turned on him and it ripped his clothes open with his tusk right from his crutch to his chest. He'd a very narrow escape. After then, that boar was never the same, you couldn't trust it. Another boar bit him in the hand between the thumb and finger. And some sows if you're not watching what you're doing when they've got young 'uns, they'll snap at you. I'd one pig yesterday [17th August] on my birthday. I put my hand in front of her in her farrowing crate and she didn't take a bit of notice. You know, she was as quiet as anything. I just put my hand in front of her nose and took a piglet away from her and she didn't snap at me. Some if you do that get very vicious. That's why mainly they have them in crates, you see, because you have to go into the pen, and you just have to touch a piglet and it'll squeal and the mother will be round on you in a minute. I once bent over putting some fresh pellets in and I touched a piglet with my foot and it squealed out and the sow nearly bit my backside, I'd to jump over the wall!

Another reason for the crates is so the sow don't lay on her little piglets. Sometimes they'll get underneath the sow and when she goes down they don't get away quick enough. Some sows are very good mothers, they'll just go down as slow as anything. Another one will just drop right down and don't care a hang.

An infra red globe hangs down on a chain over creep areas where the piglets can creep into and get completely away from the mother. The creep areas are just like little wooden and fibreglass houses with a lamp hanging through. They can come out of the hole when they want to go to their mother and have milk. They're in and out all the time, and if one starts to feed then the others all want to rush out to feed at the milk bar as well! You keep the temperature at eighty-five degrees. The infra red's just to keep the piglets warm. We did have an ultra violet fly-catcher in there once. The flies were attracted by this light and as they flew into it—snap!—they received an electric shock. It weren't very efficient. It cost £50. The Rixes saw it at the Suffolk Show three years ago. We got it on three months trial to see how we got on with it and then took it back. I've got a new spray-gun now for washing down. They saw *that* at the Suffolk Show. We're keeping it. It's a German make. You can pull the trigger and spray when and where you want with water. It's attached by electric pump to a tank of water with plenty of length of pipe. I use it mostly in the farrowing shed because, when the sows and little pigs go out, all the crates and that have to be scrubbed down and disinfected ready for the next lot to come in (one sow farrows two litters every year). The little piglets have the scours, you see, and vets tell us that if you don't scrub off thoroughly where they've dunged on the crate or on the pieces of wood the bugs can live there for a year.

The pigs for slaughter are weighed on the Monday and go off to the abattoir on the Tuesday, maybe eighteen one week, eight another. Every Monday morning I clean the muck and straw out of the feeding areas in the fattening shed so the pigs will be easier to drag along. If they've got straw and that in, they'll stick their front feet in and you can't hardly move them. You throw a little meal in, you know, just to keep them in line, then you go along and say, 'That one's going' and get hold of it by the ears and tail and drag it along to the scales in the passage-way and when the scales weigh 120, 121 right up to 130 and 140 (if they go above 140 pounds they'll come into the next weight range and fetch a lower price) I put a red cross on it with a paint stick—those pigs what are going must have a red cross on to signify they're for slaughter. The scales have a door. I shove the pig in, shut the door up. Peter standing at the other end takes the weight, puts it down in the records book, and I drag the pig out by its tail and it just turns around and goes in its pen. The same Monday we have to mark what's got to go the following week. You've got to enter the weights as well—anything from 112 right up to 119. It's only sometimes you get one or two that don't put the weight on.

Then, Tuesday morning, they've all got to be 'slapped', slap-marked on the shoulder with our number, MO 61. You use a thing with a handle that's got spikes an inch or so long with the letters and numbers on, and you press it into a pad with tattoo ink on—antiseptic so it don't cause poisoning—and give them a slap on the shoulder, *hard* so it'll take and still show when they're scrubbed. There was one chap, he slapped a pig once and he missed the pig and it went into his leg and he was numbered for life. On an MO 61 I reckon there would be between twenty and thirty points. Then

Spetchly from Cambridge come, the contractor with the lorry. He'll come between ten and eleven o'clock and we'll have all the pigs out on the loading ramp ready at ten o'clock and he'll back up, just let the tailboard down and we drive them up and off they go to the abattoir. You must not feed them on the day they go because, going on the lorry, they reckon that, being fed, some pigs are sick. You see they reckon they'll get food and that in the windpipe and it'll choke them to death. To get them to the ramp we just take them along a little passage, out the back door and drive them up into the ramp and put the tin across, and they'll stay there till the lorry comes. They're not frightened. We've got an electric prodder—you know, with two spikes on run by batteries—and give them a jab when they're a bit awkward and won't go the right way you want them. When they get to the abattoir—I've never seen it—they'll go along a passage-way. They have an electric thing to stun them, you know, on the head and then there'll be a man will hang them up and cut their throat so they bleed. Then they'll go along on hooks on rails and then a little further along there'll be somebody will scrub all the hairs off. Then a little further along there'll be somebody will open them up and take all the insides out and that. Then they're all cut in half and that and hung up and then there'll be somebody else come along and take the grades—you know, so many millimetres of fat—and if they're a certain number of millimetres of fat, then that's First Grade, you see: they get a Q.

When a pig dies on the farm I bring the tractor and forklift and just roll it on and take it down where I want to bury it in the plantation and tip it in. You must bury them at least six foot deep. If you don't you can get fined. If it's too big to bury the Hunt comes with a truck and takes it away to the kennels for dogmeat. At Norman's we had cows struck by lightning. They've come home scorched and a few hours after they've died. They went to the Hunt too. I don't believe in hunting. The Normans never had the Hunt on their farm at all, not the whole thirteen years I was down there. Mr Rix doesn't hunt either. Foxes can be shot—one year when I was down at Brundon we shot seven. Or else they can be gassed—you shove a cannister down the hole and bung it up afterwards—but I prefer shooting. You can do rabbits just the same but there aren't so many about now since they had that myxomatosis round about 1969. I don't mind shooting at all. I've shot rabbits and birds myself. The hounds rip the fox to pieces. It's not humanely killed first. The hounds will even take a domestic animal. If they run through a yard and they see a cat or anything, they'll have it, they'll rip it to pieces . . .

In the morning, after the pigs, I go outside into the fields if the weather is fine—if it's not fine I do repairs in the tractor shed—and leave off work half past twelve to half past one for dinner at home, say, tomato, lettuce and ham, bread and butter and two cups of tea; the meals vary from day to day.

In the tractor shed, for instance, we've been getting the sugar beet harvester ready. In the course of a season the chains can get right slack and you've to take out some of the trace-links to tighten them up. Then you've got to sharpen the knives so as to have nice blades for cutting the sugar beet tops off. Then you have to put the wheels out to a hundred and five inches for going round the headlands (when you've got your headlands done you've got to put them in again to ninety-five inches to go up and down the rows). Or you can repair the trailers. If the wood's gone rotten we rip it off, put new wood on. Any iron what's been rusted away we cut it all off with an acetylene cutter—we've got all our own welding equipment. I don't do any welding myself, but I might hold a new angle in place while the others weld it. Else I'll be creosoting the boards in any of the sheds so they last longer. They reckon creosote is good for whooping cough done in a different formula. Same as terramycin—that can be used on human beings as well as animals but in a different formula; Judith had it when she had pneumonia and bronchitis. For the pigs you just add twelve teaspoonfuls to three gallons of water when they're thin and poorly. It can be used for cows, pigs, fish, birds or anything.

Outside we're now harvesting the wheat. I should reckon we got sixteen to eighteen tonnes off one field of six acres. You see with this metric business they don't go in tons now, they go in tonnes. A tonne is about 40lbs less than a ton. The boss, Mr Rix, he'll drive the combine hisself because nobody else likes the driving of it, not really. One of the boys will be carting the corn away into the grain store where it goes into twenty-ton bins. We've got twenty of them. This year there'll be about six bins of barley and the rest will be wheat. There'll be one of us driving a tractor with a baler behind it and baling the straw up. The bales fall onto a sledge behind the baler, about a dozen to fifteen bales a time. The bales slide out and I'm walking behind setting them up into heaps, you know, twenty-one to a heap. After we've got a field of bales done another tractor will come and pick them up, one twenty-one at the front and another twenty-one at the back. Then off it goes to the Dutch barn where we're stacking the straw. I do most of the stacking because the boys don't like heights.

Because this August is turning out wet Peter and Trevor and me are going behind breaking up the fields with the cultivators and chisel plough to kill all the weeds before drilling the winter corn in the middle of October. We've fitted the drill up with tramlines for spraying and fertilising. We've fertiliser in the drill when the corn is being sown. Then in the spring when, you know, it's beginning to grow we put more top dressing on and within a fortnight or so you can see a vast difference, you know, between where you've done and where you haven't—one lot of corn will be two or three inches taller.

The sugar beet harvest is at the end of September,

beginning of October. The harvester's a Standen Cyclone, self-propelled. You pull a lever and the machinery starts working. I shall be waiting at the end of a row with my tractor and highlift trailer—it's all tractors with Mr Rix; I'd sooner walk up and down a field all day long with a horse. I *usually* wait at the end of a row but if the rows are too long and he gets his tank full before he gets to the end of the row I follow him and draw up beside him. He'll stop and pull a lever and that starts an elevator thing what come over the trailer and the sugar beet will come up a trace into the trailer. Then I cart it back to the pad to pile it. You lift the trailer to the height you want it—it'll lift as high as our bedroom window, that's twelve to thirteen feet—, pull your lever over and that'll tip the trailer up so it shoots the beet out the back. We pile it on a big cement place with a brick wall on the back so when we're loading it onto the lorry to go to the sugar beet factories we don't push it out of the way. If there's a severe frost or anything we put bales of straw on top as a protection. The sugar beet factories open in September. When you've got a few loads, the contractor—Mr Hunt from Sicklesmere—comes and takes them away, his drivers take them in to Bury. If a load's too dirty he'll send it back. Every farmer that grows sugar beet gets so many permits per season. We've got thirty-five acres of sugar beet and I reckon between forty and fifty permits, nine to fourteen tonnes to a lorry-load, that's one permit. Wednesdays is our day for loading.

Wintertime, if it's dry outside, I shall be cutting up wood. We've got a lot to cut down this year that's had Dutch Elm Disease, about thirty, I reckon. They'll all be cut for firewood. Mr Rix lets us have a trailer-load, and my father-in-law, he'll give him some as well.

When the spring come along, between March and April, we could be tilling the ground ready for the spring corn—the spring barley and spring wheat—making it cultivated and rotaried and harrowed and sprayed for wild oats and black grass before it's drilled. Then it'll all be harrowed up again and drilled with fertiliser on, and when the corn come through in about three weeks that'll be rolled when it's about two or three inches high, and as the corn gets higher that'll be sprayed for different kinds of weeds such as may weed and thistles and fat hen and hog grass. Then between March and April time the sugar beet fields will be pulled down with Dutch harrows all ready for drilling. There's a lot to do to that. The fields will be sprayed to kill the weeds, then pulled up again till you get a nice smooth bed, then that'll have agricultural salt put on and 6 cwt. of artificial manure per acre and harrowed up again. Then Mr Rix comes behind with the sugar beet drill and the band sprayer on and, as the sugar beet is sown in the rows, so the spray will go along on the top of the row behind to kill any surface weeds, and after that we shall do the top dressing of the winter corn and the rolling of it and after the sugar beet has got two to three leaves on we shall be 'chopping out', nine inches apart—you're supposed to leave eighty to eighty-five sugar beet every twenty-two yards. Then the sugar beet is all tractor-hoed and left and then any rogue beet a-growing—that's the sugar beet that's very small and runs straight up to seed—, they've to be all pulled out.

We use Paraquat spring and summer when we're killing weeds. You must keep it locked away; it's very dangerous. A year or so ago it was on the wireless and in the paper that this woman, she went to a chemist place, you know, and bought it—you have to sign a Poisons Book for it—and she brought it home and gave it to her husband in cups of tea. They took him off to hospital and he died, you know, in great pain. It's a very slow and agonising death. The recording chap at Norman's when he took the milk samples, he had little pink tablets in his bottles and *they* could kill. He used to have a sort of ammunition case like they had in the war and he had to padlock it every night with the bottles of samples in because he had to leave it behind and come next morning to take another sample to go in the same bottle. But there was an antidote for it—it was writ on the box like for the doctor on account of children and that.

June we'll be repairing and attending to the buildings and cleaning out the grain store ready for the harvest in July and August, cleaning all the bins out, getting rid of all the bugs—the beetles and bean weevils and wheat weevils and all suchlike. Sometimes we use smoke bombs. I reckon we've ninety acres of wheat, mostly feeding wheat some of which *can* be used for milling, and about fifty acres of barley. There's malting barley and there's feeding barley. After everything is combined, we shall bale say about four thousand bales of straw. This year we just want to do some barley straw because we have about four hundred bales of wheat straw left over from last year. We tried to sell them but nobody wanted them. All the wheat straw will be burned.

When we're burning the straw what we do first of all is to turn the straw in away from the hedges with a swath-turner. Then a chap will come round with a tractor and cultivator and break all up round the headland. The headland is right the way round the outside of a field, about twenty-five feet. We burn all the headland up first, then the whole lot of us go into the field different ways, setting fire to all the rows. You've got to be very careful you don't get trapped and that the wind's blowing away from buildings. This field outside Clapstile Cottage is about thirty-five acres. On a good day when it's all nice and dry that'll be all gone in about five minutes. You can see the hares running out of the way and the pheasants flying up, squawking. There was one year a hedge got scorched and there were some pigeons in it and they could hardly flap their wings, they were so hot. One year, poor dears . . . Peter and I, we trimmed a hedge up and had a heap of all this old hedgerow and sticks to burn and we set fire to it and all at once we heard squealing and two rabbits runned out right black. They got to their holes before we could kill them. Their fur and that was smoking as they runned along . . .

It varies but usually I go in now at about four o'clock again to feed the pigs. If they want a bit of clean straw in the farrowing shed I put it in and I have a look round to see if there's any to farrow at night. You can always tell because they've got a little milk. Then I may go back between ten and twelve o'clock to see if they're all right and, if there's any starting to farrow, well I have to stay there.

I come home normally five o'clock, have a cup of tea and feed the rabbits and if there's any job to do like sawing wood or cutting nettles down I'll do that. A year or so ago I was indoors on holiday—I get three weeks April, June—and Cynthia in the morning she always feeds the rabbits, she went outside and called me, she say, 'Len! There's a rabbit dead!' I say, '*Rabbit* dead! Why?! How?' She say, 'Come and have a look!' It was all battered about the head; the head was completely crushed. We phoned from Mrs Campbell's and had the police out. They said, 'If it happens again give us a ring and we'll keep an eye out.' It hasn't happened again but we've an idea it was a poacher chap who's always hanging about here and there all hours of the night. He may have been going to take it and been disturbed, you see. Inside the door of the box was pressed his finger tips, you know, where they were spattered with blood.

Between seven and eight o'clock we'll have tea, say lamb chops, potatoes, green peas or instead of peas we'll have cabbage or celery or leeks. Sometimes we have Yorkshire pudding first of all. Then we have a jam roly-poly followed by a cup of tea. Or we might have a sponge pudding or rice pudding and fruit or custard and fruit. No matter what's on, we switch off the television before Judith goes to bed and all sit round the table and say our prayers. Each of us all say one round, you know, make them up as we go along. Like we'd say, 'Thank You, Lord, for bringing us safe through this day.

Thank You for our daily work and giving us the strength to go about our daily duties. And may You keep us safe throughout the night hours. Amen.' My in-laws, they say prayers at night just the same. We don't say them in the morning; we're up and doing in the morning with all the animals to feed. Judith will go to bed at ten to half past and my wife will go half past eleven time. I'll be watching the television till close-down. I ain't all that heavy a sleeper; though I get up early in the morning and go to bed late I just can't sleep. Sometimes I've been up from six o'clock in the morning till five o'clock the next morning when the pigs are farrowing. Sows are like a woman, they like to have their children at night. We take it in turns. If I've had two or three nights running then somebody else will do it.

Last year I had two gilts die on me. It was terrifically hot and there was too much stress for them and they just died; there was nothing I could do about it. A pig is a gilt till she's had her first litter, then she's called a sow. Like the cows—till they've had their first calf they're heifers. When you see 'Maiden Heifers for Sale' you know they haven't calved. They call a woman a maiden, don't they, until she's had children?

Chapter Ten

About five years ago there was an Old Time Rally in Long Melford—old fashioned cars, steam engines, aeroplanes. Very interesting. And this May there was the South Suffolk Show at Bridge Street Farm—Mr Colson's. But in Alpheton there usually isn't enough to do. On June the 11th for the Jubilee we had races and fancy dress for children five to ten years old on the lawns up at The Old Rectory by kind permission of Mr and Mrs Morris. (Alpheton Church hasn't got a rector now, it just has visiting preachers.) Judith as she's fourteen helped with the races, seeing who came in first. Then there was a party for young and old and everybody in the Dutch barn at Mr Graham and Mr Alec Maskell's—Tye Farm, arable and chickens. One or two of the villagers got together with a jumble sale and raised the money. There was a barn dance and food and licence for a bar. We didn't go.

The old school used to be the Village Hall. After the teachers died off in about 1933 all the Alpheton children, including my wife—she was five at the time; she'll be fifty next February—they had to go to the school at Shimpling. Then these latter years it went to rack and ruin and somebody bought it and converted it into a dwelling. The villagers could have done it up theirselves; it was their own fault. Same as with Chestnut Cottages. My father-in-law's father bought the whole three cottages for £20 and sold them about 1924 for

£100 to the postman. He changed the name to Sunset Cottages. There used to be a pretty mess around there and it was empty for a while. Finally a complete stranger called Mrs Leven bought them and knocked them together—at least I *think* it was she done most of the renovating—round about 1970 and changed the name to Woodhall and sold it last year for £22,000, or that's what I heard. Fifty years ago, the rector of Alpheton offered to loan my father-in-law £200 to buy the house next door to us where Mrs Campbell lives with her friend Mrs Gibby. It now must be worth about £22,000 like the other one. They got rid of the thatch and had the roof tiled for over a thousand pound. Because he used to work for Mr Rix my father- and mother-in-law still live in Buxton's Cottage which was tied to Clapstile Farm. He's to pay a rent now, of course—I think it's eight pound a week. It's a bit steep but Mr Rix reckons he could make thousands out of that house though it's years and years old. It's difficult for shopping and that but they have SPAR come round from Cockfield to deliver and we get goods for them when we go to Sudbury or Melford on a Saturday. There's no village store or post office in the village at all now! We've been fighting for them but we still can't get them. All we've got is Fred Elliott's garage and Alpheton Garage and Transport Café.

This year being Jubilee Year there should be a Village Hall being built in the near future. There ain't a lot of people interested but Cynthia and myself are thinking about it. She wants to run a young people's club and have darts, snooker, table tennis, dominoes, cards . . . sports and that first, then have a cup of coffee and talk to them on the Bible. There's several villages do that now. There's the Assembly Hall at Waldingfield—the Brethren; you know, not the strict Brethren, just the ordinary Brethren. They've been getting between thirty and forty children in a week. While they're having their coffee and hotdogs and biscuits after their sports and all that they'll have a talk about Jesus and the Bible. It's really working: they're showing great interest. We'd have a free will offering—you know, a plate or a glass bowl at the door—and people could drop a coin in if they felt free to do so as they went out. Otherwise we'd pay from the Mission Room funds. You could have religious films; have a bit of fun with ordinary films first and have the religious films afterwards. I could hire a 16 mm. film projector from Sudbury. I went down and inquired once and you could hire the projector and the screen for four pound for the night. Then a film might cost eight pound on top of that. It's not all that cheap really. We had a film once in the old school—'Martin Luther'—and that cost twelve pound.

We pay ten pound a year for the Mission Room in Bridge Street to Mr Dick Ruffle. He's retired now. He used to be a miller, do pig foods and poultry foods. To the best of my knowledge his father, Mr W. J. Ruffle, decided in about 1910 that he wanted a Free church in Bridge Street instead of a little hut in Alpheton, and that's how the Mission Room started—in a store shed, sitting round on sacks of beans. It's stayed in the Ruffle family ever since. Mrs Rix was Joan Ruffle, the daughter of Mr Dick's brother Hammond. When they was first married Mr Rix used to keep the Post Office at Whepstead, but by the time I was courting Cynthia they was at Clapstile. We went to Hammond Ruffle's funeral service in Melford United Reformed Church the day after we moved to Clapstile. Joan Tricker who plays the organ now lives in the Mill which was his brother Dick's house. Her husband's a television engineer and she does bed and breakfast. Before them it was a Mr and Mrs Kenny. Mr Dick Ruffle had a bungalow built further up the hill about ten years ago. He don't come into the Mission Room any more but he still rents it to us and we can have it as long as we want it. We added the vestry ourselves. It came in sections from away up in London. It's only just the tin part's his. If he wanted the place back he'd have to buy the vestry off us or else we'd take it down. It cost over £100 to do. We asked him first and he said, 'Go ahead!'

Since I was healed and that, I'm feeling that I'm being called by God to the Healing Ministry, and when I'm about down in the town and I see people in wheel-chairs and even when I'm feeding the pigs a voice keeps saying to me, 'I want you to go into the Healing Ministry.' It's as if the Lord is speaking to me in my mind. I've taken three services now down at the Mission Room and every time I preach there I've got an urge to heal. The wife and I are praying, we're hoping to go all out for Healing Meetings at the Mission Room. My advertisements could go in *The Suffolk Free Press* and the Parish Magazine. The woman who does the Parish Magazine will put anything in for the village: anything you want she'll put in. I'd say, 'Divine Healing and Praise Meetings to be held at Bridge Street Mission Room such and such a day of such and such a month, you know, conducted by Len Mills or whoever.' We'd invite other ministers and speakers like Mo Baldry to come along—Mo's a teacher in electrics at Ipswich College. You don't have to have a special permit or anything. The Church of England or the Roman Catholic Church won't allow a layman to heal, not someone the same as ourselves like. But the others will except for the Brethren who don't have healing meetings because they don't believe in them. There's the Apostolic; there's the Free Church; there's the United Reformed, the Methodist, the Presbyterian and the Assemblies of God. We'd have hymns, choruses, prayer, then an appeal for anybody to come out to love the Lord Jesus. Then the second part would be the Healing Ministry. What you do is ask is anybody suffering from illnesses like rheumatics, headaches, nervous disorders, T.B. to come forward if they wish and we pray for them. I'll place my hands on their head and pray aloud. Sometimes they fall straight to the ground. The Spirit of God is working in them, you see, and they fall down under the Spirit. A man stands behind the person you're praying for so if they fall down under the Spirit he can ease them down—so they don't fall and hurt theirselves, you see. You can have someone else praying and doing the laying on of hands if you want to. The healer is prayed for first so that the Lord will dwell in him and work through him as he does it. If someone is deaf you place your hands on his ears—or they've got bad eyesight you place your fingers on the eyes—and pray for them. You say, 'Lord, unstop this deaf ear!' and then you snap your fingers and say, 'Can you hear that?' or you say, 'Can you hear my watch ticking?' Sometimes they say, 'Yes, I can!' and everybody will call out, 'Praise the Lord!', you know. Some of the congregation are praying aloud and some quietly. They can be speaking in tongues and nobody understands it. They can be speaking in Spanish, German or Arabic—it just comes to them. If the Spirit invites him, the healer will speak in a foreign tongue as well. Trevor Dearing was once trying to reform a prostitute and, as he was praying for her, all she kept saying was, 'Jesus is not alive! He's dead!' And Trevor kept saying, 'He's not dead! He's alive! He's alive!' She kept fighting against it and he still kept on, and all at once she passed right out on the floor. She was lying on the floor for five minutes and when she spoke afterwards she was a different person altogether, she was right happy.

If I got a job near Sudbury we could still come to the Mission Room. If I got a job somewhere further away we'd find out before we went if there are any Free churches and chapels or anything like that in the district. And if I was requested to go anywhere—town, village—I'd just go. The church or chapel would tell me the dates of their Divine Healing and I'd send back the dates when I could go and it would be put on the posters. After I was seen at meetings healing people, I'd be invited everywhere; it would be in the press and everything. Wherever else it is we go to live I shall try to get permission to do healing meetings. The committee will sit to decide if they'll allow it and then give me the go ahead. Eventually when my father-in-law and mother-in-law pass on and Charlie passes on—they're all old what's there in the Mission Room now except for us three youngsters: Judith, Cynthia and me—it'll have to close anyway; there won't be enough contributions to pay the expenses—the electricity, the rent, the painting inside and outside.

Before you came we were anticipating moving and we still are really, you know. Mr Rix knows that we're trying; I've told him I'll go when the right job come along. We're looking out in *The East Anglian Daily Times* and in *The Suffolk Free Press* on Thursdays, the *The Bury Free Press*, that's Fridays. We're looking for a job with a bigger house and a nice garden, you see. Because of Peter's bungalow our garden's finished. Losing our garden was what really 'got our goat' as we say in Suffolk. In the little bit that's left of it a trench was dug all the way along, we'd to move all the rabbit hutches out of the way for the men laying the pipes to link up with ours and go down, you know, to the main sewer beds. It's now been about five weeks and it hasn't been filled in properly *yet* [23rd August]. It's all been inspected and passed. I don't know what's holding them up. This year I wanted to have my holiday in the summer when Judith was having hers but since they've started on the bungalow Peter isn't available to do the pigs.

I'll always stay with pigs. I'd like to stay with them till I die if possible. I've got so used to them now, I love them. I can't get no higher. I'm in sole charge: I'm on my own. I shouldn't mind working with them full time. Then you know what you're a-doing of, you know. I applied for a job with pigs at Folly Road Farm, Mildenhall, just the other side of Bury. The farm manager came over to see us. The wages there was £50 a week plus overtime. I'd have been seeing after three hundred dry sows—you know, those that have pigged—full-time as part of a team of six. One man would be in charge of the farrowing shed, another man in charge of something else.

He say, 'We've got good houses. If you want a man to do his work properly, tip-top like, you've got to give him a good house and pay him well.' But there's an aerodrome at Mildenhall, an American air base with big jets carrying American personnel. It would have been too noisy for Cynthia with her migraines; she wouldn't have been able to put up with it. Which is a pity because she could have got plenty of café work as it's near a town. She *loves* being a waitress and that.

To live you want a house in good condition. The condition of this house is poor. Downstairs is as damp as anything. The governor should keep it in repair. We'd to wait over a year for a window to be put in—it was rotting right away. It was nearly falling out when he finally did it. If it had been left any longer it *would* have fell out. Then the rain was coming in under the door. We had to tell him about *that*. You have to really keep getting on to him before he'll do anything. He's supposed to be getting us the weather-boarding for a new shed where the wood and bicycle and garden tools are. I don't know when that'll be, I'm sure. At Mr Norman's it was different again. I used to be afraid to ask for anything to be done. He used to say when the wife went up, 'Why on earth don't Len tell me?! I shan't bite his head off!' He gave me a dressing down for not telling him. He say, 'If there's anything you want done, Len, just tell me. I live comfortably,' he say, 'and I want my chaps to live comfortably. It's no good you sitting in the house,' he say, 'and there's water and that coming through the ceiling or there's water coming into the window,' he say. 'It's no good at all,' he say. 'You've got to just tell me,' he say, 'and I'll have it done' He'd had all the house done up and water was still coming in the window. There was a little bit wrong somewhere and I left it and left it and left it and eventually Cynthia saw him and told him about it. He got really nasty over it, you know. He said 'Why didn't you tell me?!'

Instead of the two bedrooms, bathroom, kitchen and front room we've got here, we'd like a kitchen and a place, you know, where you have your meals and that in, and a lounge like, you know, what they call a front room, and three bedrooms and, you know, a bathroom and toilet all in one like, you know, and a nice big garden—I wouldn't mind half an acre. You always have to bring all your own furniture and everything to these tied places. We've an electric cooker. I bought that myself. The Rayburn to heat the water was already here. That's all. There's some jobs you *do* get a place that's already furnished if you need it, for instance a housekeeper or a butler when his wife is the maid or cook in a house like Kentwell Hall or Melford Hall. Well perhaps only at Melford Hall: the woman who runs that, she's a Lady.

18th August

It rained late on the night of the 16th and all yesterday and today. Mr Rix and one of the boys were combining on the 16th until a quarter to ten at night but it's been too wet since to bale the straw. It's got terribly wet and we'll have to come later with the straw turner and turn it over and dry it out, which takes the biggest part of a day. The rain's going to make us a bit later with the harvest—you know, maybe two or three weeks—but the wheat will be all the better for it because it'll make it swell. It's a lot easier now, with all the modern farm machinery, if the corn gets laid. On your cutter bar at the front of the combine you've got lifters so, as you're going along, they lift the barley or the wheat so you can cut it. It'll want more drying when it'll come into the grain store, that's all. We've got five drying bins, but if it's a nice, really hot time you don't need to dry the grain at all, you just take it straight to the ordinary bins. As the wheat or barley is dried out, it goes by conveyor into the ordinary bins, then at the end of the harvest you fill up the drying bins for ordinary storing. Some years we grow more wheat and some years we grow more barley, so the number of bins for each varies. You have to vice versa. If you grow the same crop on the same ground every year, you get less and less and less because the ground gets sick of it. Some of the corn will stay in store till next June, July time. You know, it just depends on the price. If the price is high we get rid of it quick. Last year wheat was over £80 a tonne. One year it went up to £84 a tonne—and that's only for 20 cwt.! With all the equipment—the augers and conveyors and that—you can load fourteen tonne on a lorry in an hour.

Tonight Cynthia's gone to the doctor to see if she's got cancer of the cervix. She didn't want to go. But that's just a simple thing, that is: they can soon operate on *that*! I look on the bright side of things. She looks on the dark side of things.

22nd August

Today's been a tiring day because of the bad weather. We'd to get the drain rods out and pull them through the pipes in the ditches round the fields blocked up with leaves and rubbish and that; the water couldn't get away. We should be all right here but other areas have had worse than what we have. If the corn gets laid on the ground too long it starts to grow up again: you know, the corn inside the ears takes root.

24th August

Today it was still raining, the position was grave. The wheat was beginning to turn black. Another week of rain and it'll be no good for milling, only for animal feed. Rain doesn't affect the barley which goes mostly for malting and animal feed, so that's O.K. I was helping combine it today till the rain got too heavy—there's only another twenty acres to do. The rain's good for the sugar beet. It makes them grow bigger and they're easier to lift out when they're wet, you don't snap the tap-root where most of the sugar is.

Yesterday, 24 cwt. of barley seedcorn arrived for sowing in mid-October if the land is ready and chisel-ploughed. But the late harvest may prevent this.

26th August
The weather's been fine today and we've been harvesting. We finished the barley. All we've got to do now is the wheat. If it's fine we'll do some tomorrow. About five or six acres won't be a lot of good—that'll have to be put aside for cattle feeding. The rest is fairly good and if the weather stays fine for a week we shall be finished. But if it rains again we'll lose the lot; it'll begin to grow again inside the husk. Then it'll only be fit to be sent away for feeds; it'll be kaput.

5th August, 1980
Cynthia's visit to the doctor raised no alarms, and the harvest was, in fact, saved—wheat was actually up one tonne per acre on Summer, 1976. But, in October, 1977, due to matters personal to the parties alone, Mr Rix was obliged to terminate Len's employment, and the family now lives in Long Melford. Judith has left school and controls a mat-making machine in a Sudbury factory. Cynthia, as principal breadwinner, works Mondays to Saturdays for Social Services as a 'home help', and, during term-time, is a school bus-attendant. Because of asthma and weak legs, Len has never found another employer. At home, however, he practises his love of animals among forty hens, seventeen rabbits, four budgerigars, two canaries, two guinea pigs, four hamsters, one dog, four mice and fourteen cats. And, though he has not pursued his ambition to become a healer, the usual meetings at the Mission Room continue against all odds. Editor.

Appendix

Due to a stroke suffered in 1972 at the age of seventy (see pp 89 and 90), Albert Edward Mitchell, 'Oiky's' father-in-law, former grave-digger of Alpheton Church, and cattle and pig stockman at Clapstile Farm during several generations, was unable to complete this account of Alpheton remembered. It was written neatly in a blue covered, blue-lined exercise book. No amendments have been made to it of any kind, except a one of 'Arthurs' to 'Andrewes' (p 166).

Alpheton,
'As I remember it,'
by
A. E. Mitchell

'Preface,'

As I am a Native of Alpheton, being bred, and born in it, I have been asked by one or two Residents, who have moved into this little more than a hamlet, in recent years, to write a book, in regards to the Life, and History of it, as I remember it, since the Year of Our Lord, Nineteen Hundred. And so, I will do my best during the dark evenings of this winter, Nineteen Seventy, to record faithfully, and as far as possible, accurately, the History, changing events, and Life, as I remember it, of Alpheton, being partly assisted by my Sister, Elizabeth, in the hope that it will be of interest, and perhaps help, to anyone residing in the Village now, or at any time hereafter. I therefore dedicate, my writings to:—

The Peoples of the Village of Alpheton,
my Beloved, and Native Home.

A.E.M.

Alpheton, a little scattered Village, containing just over Two Hundred Souls, and being an entirely agricultural project at the commencement of my remembrances, brings to my mind many happy memories, and of course, intermingled sad ones as well, not forgetting the Humorous side, of which I will record, as I go along. It contained a lovely old Church, (and still does,) a Public house and a forge, both of which have now been discarded, and sold, a tiny Post office, and stores, A Rectory, now sold, and occupied as a Private Residence, a School, now used as a Village Hall, and at one time, a Pork Butcher, also, a Miller, and Corn Merchant, The Land of the Village being divided into eight farms, known by the following Names: Alpheton Hall, Tye Farm, Green Farm, Clapstile Farm, Buxtons Farm, Red Lion Farm and Pub combined, Elms Farm, and Mansers Farm, and approximately forty five acres of Tithle Land, belonging to the Incumbrant of the Rectory. Life was hard, but happy, wages were low, and the working hours long, consisting of a six day week, often in many cases, commencing at Six, a.m. and finishing Six p.m., however life was accepted for what it was, and a happy fellowship existed among Employer and employee.

Well, let us take a look first of All, at the Church of St Peter, and St Paul, built to the Glory of God, and has a record of Rectors from the Year of Grace, twelve Hundred, but during repairs, of which I will speak in a few moments, the Workmen found, high up in the inside of the Tower, the date, Eleven Hundred, which takes its erection further back still. The church yard, having been used for a great many years, as a resting place for mortal remains became full, and was therefore closed for Burials, and an extension was granted by the Bishop, and a piece of land given (a portion known as the croft,) for the use of a Burial ground, by a Mr Leonard Makins, owner of the Hall Farm, this peice of ground was consecrated by the Bisop of the diocese in June 1923, having been enclosed around by iron railings, the first person to be buried on this new ground was a Mr Patrick Rose, father of Mrs Elijah Andrews, of No. 4, Council Cottages, I remember during the day in which my father was digging the grave for his resting place, A Mr William Moatt came and looked in, exclaiming, you've got a hard job there Sam, little knowing that shortly afterwards my father would be preparing *his* next door. This new burial ground, and directly behind it, is the site upon which the Danes of Olden days fought their battles, evidence, and proof of this, is borne out by the trenches for the Infantry, until recently, being seen quite clearly running alongside the (now enclosed) Churchyard, and also by the finding of several small pony shoes, about eighteen inches below the Surface of the Soil, and of course, human remains (bones) together with pony jawbones etc, which my father, and afterwards I myself have found. So much for the Churchyard which my father and I kept tidy for a great many years, by cutting it with a scythe, and weeding the paths three times each year, for the princely sum of thirty shillings, but we thought little of the money, we did it as a devotion, and love for the Church, one thing I must tell you before we go inside the sacred building, and that is, during the years, of which the Revd Bartrum was the incumbrant, up both sides of each of the two paths were rows of Standard Rose trees, approximately thirty altogether in number, these briars were local ones from the hedgerows of Alpheton, and grafted with fragrant rose buds from the Rectory garden by my father, these giving a beautiful display of flowers all through the Summer months, whilst encircling the trysting gate, was a lovely pink bush rose, giving a fragrant welcome to the worshippers, as they entered, the main gate never being opened only for weddings and funerals, now let us look inside, where we shall see quite a number of changes. In the belfry are two bells, there used to be four, but I do not remember them, as two were sold many years ago, to provide seating in the church, evidence of the presence of these four bells, is seen by the four holes in the first floor, through which the ropes passed, from the bell tongues down into the vestry beneath, one old verger is reported to have rung all four bells himself, for divine worship on Sundays, sitting in a chair, and ringing each one in succession, and in Rhymn, by having a bell rope in each hand, and one on each foot in a stirrup like clasp, but this I cannot verify, as it was before my birth. Coming out of the Vestry door, and looking into the empty space above it, there used to be a window there similar to the East Window, with coloured glass paintings, almost the same pattern, but it became deteriorated over the years, and has since been removed, leaving less Beauty to this otherwise delightful interior, the beams of the ceiling of the Church Body which are now to be seen, were originally covered with lath and Mortar Plaster, thus providing a dome shaped ceiling, being snow white in colour, blending with the side walls, and causing a lighter effect than now, one can see where the wooden laths were nailed to the wooden beams of the ceiling structure, although the beams were varnished, having travelled from the vestry, and along the ceiling, we come to the chancel roof interior, which remains unchanged over the years, and now we descend, and take a look at the Alter, this beautiful piece of craftsmanship, replaced the former Alter, which was previously the Communion table, now standing on the right hand side of the Sanctuary, the New Alter being provided in the early years of His Incumbrancy, by the Revd Bartrum, the Reader will agree with me, that this is a magnificent gesture of devotion to the Glory of God, as it stands in its sacred Position. before we journey down the isle, we must take a look at the lovely lamps which provide the lighting during the winter months, believe it or not dear reader, before they were placed in the church, the lighting was provided by six little double burner parafin oil lamps, three hanging on either side of the Church body, the Chancel lighting consisted of two candlesticks placed on the Alter, these small lamps held one and a half pints of parafin each, giving the reader some idea of the lighting effect, but who minded, we were there to worship God, and if we could not see to read, we sang and recited by heart, and all for the Glory, and love of God. The lovely Brass hanging Lamps which now adorn the Church, and are now almost worn out, were purchased, and placed in the Church in the year 1909-10, The two in the Chancel came first, and were equipped with two white globes, these were afterwards replaced by two green ones, to throw the light down upon the Choir stalls, next came the two large ones in the Church body, bought from a large London firm, and gave a magnificent light, but sad to record, the lower Lamp, after a few years of service, had the misfortune to break the hanging chain, and crashed to the floor, a new chain was purchased, and the present white globe, was given by Mr T Colson's Mother, who lived then in the adjoining Hall farm, but it received injuries from which it never really recovered, although it has remained in faithful service down to the present time. The small red Globed lamp in the chancel immediately above the Alter rails was placed in its hanging position as the last one to complete the five altogether. in its decorated brass hanger, is the body of the lamp, into which the parafin is placed, and which is actually a one lb Lyles Golden Syrup tin, turned inside out, into the top of this is screwed the burner and should be fitted with a small glass, but after the original first Chimney broke, it could not be fitted with another, as none could be found small enough. These beautiful lamps have been admired by many over the years, and it will be observed that they were placed in the position to form the design of the Cross, so that those who came to worship were always beneath the Symbol of Christs sacrifice for mankind, in later years, four small brass candlesticks joined the former two on the Alter front, also placed before the Alter rails are two tall wooden Candle sticks, in memory of a Debenham Family and given by Relatives who lived in the village many years back, and who are all laid to rest, in a row, the whole family, eight in number, in the old Church yard, immeadiately to the left of the Porch, on the small plot, these candlesticks came into the Churchs possession in the year, 1908 and stands one on each side, left, and right, no prettier sight can be seen anywhere, when the five lamps, and the eight Candles are all alight, it is facinating to behold. we linger again in the chancel for a moment, and there we see a change, for in the early years of the nineteen hundreds, two large choir stalls stood, one on either side, where now stands the smaller ones, with end heads like the others ones still there, these heads were removed when these former stalls were removed and are now fitted, one on each front seat in the body of the Church, stepping down from the chancel, we notice the Pulpit has changed sides, formerly standing just behind the Lectern, but was moved over by the Revd Williamson, in 1935, to its original place, where it now stands, (during structural repairs,) the Pulpit used to have what was known as a sounding board, to throw the Preachers voice down to the People, this hung by two chains from the wooden rail, that runs along the top of the left wall, and Ceiling, the two hooks are still there, from which it was suspended, and can be clearly seen, where the Pulpit now stands, was the site of the American Organ, which provided the accomponiment for the Services, and was played efficiently, and regularly, whatever the weather, by a young man from Long Melford, but more of that later, just behind the organ, and immediately in front of the Congregation, was the heating arrangement, being a huge tortoise stove, this would consume a large amount of coke fuel, but effectively warmed the Church from this position, to shield the heat from the organist, an asbestos screen was purchased, and placed in between stove and organist, and remained in use until about 1925, parts of it are now used to cover up a newly dug grave before a funeral, the present seating replaced the old fashioned pews, some of which were retained, and are in position, as they were, behind the main door at the rear of the church. at the extreme bottom, where the Harmonium now stands, was the Vergers pew, (my Fathers), attached to the wall, was a book shelf into which, all the Prayer, and Hymn books, had to [be] placed each Sunday evening, this was beside the Vergers pew, and woe betide anyone, who distributed books from that shelf, apart from the Verger, this was his duty, and responsibility. we come now to the font, standing in front of the Vestry Door, this is its original position, never having been moved, it formerly contained an old cover, which was chained to the interior of the rim, and fastened to a staple, but was removed in 1910, the old cover having been gone several years previously, the cover that it now contains was placed thereon in 1910 by the Revd Bartrum, in memory of King Edward the 7th and the writer of this Book, is proud to say, that in the absence of a London Architect, who could not get down, I was chosen to sketch, and design it myself, imagine dear reader, my joy, at the age of nine, to see my sketching accepted and used, in the structure of this lovely Cover, one will notice at the Base of the font, are two marks on the floor, one in front, and one at the Rear, this is where there were two small raised steps placed, the rear one was for the Rector to stand on, when Christening a baby, and the front step was to hold a Brass ewer containing water for the Christening Ceremony, each step was covered by a small blue mat, turning again as we stand in the Aisle, on our left main Wall, can be seen a large portrait of St Christopher, who is carrying the Christ Child on his Shouler over a stream, how far back this dates from, when the Picture was engraved upon this wall, is unknown, as no knowledge of its existence there was known, until the Revd Bartrum during his incumbrancy 1900–1916, had the walls to the Church interior, scraped for decorating purposes, and it was then uncovered, and revealed, but one has to be very clear sighted to observe all its details, which include of course the pebbles in the stream of water, and fish, St Christopher holds a staff in one hand, and the Holy Child and orb, surmounted with a Cross in His hand, in order to preserve this originally beautiful scene, the Revd Bartrum had it covered by a green curtain, with two cords attached to a brass runner, one to uncover the picture for visitors to view, and the other to recover it again, but after a few years of Service, this curtain was removed, and taken away, as it was felt, it was brushing the wall, and therefore causing damage far more, than if the picture remained in the daylight, one thought more concerning the Church furniture, and for this we travel again to the Alter, upon which stands the lovely brass Cross. this was the gift of the Revd Bartrum, which became the successor of a small white painted wooden Cross which had hithertoo occupied the Centre of the Alter. The large iron gate at the entrance to the Church-yard, was also in remembrance of the Late King Edward 7th a small iron plaque in its centre, bore the letters E.R. but has recently disappeared. We now take a look at the Porch of Entrance to this Beautiful old Church, dedicated as it is to St Peter, and St Paul, as can be seen by a framed picture hanging on the left-wall as one enters, the Porch, it was in a very poor Structural state, the outside door was in one piece, and consisted of a rough wooden frame, with its interior filled with thin wire, letting in of course the prevailing weather, the rain would beat through and run across the floor into the Church causing damage, as also the fog in Winter months, however, the entire structure of the Porch was renovated by the Builder, Mr Theobald of Long Melford, under the orders of the Revd Bartrum, who had many outside Friends who contributed to the Cost, The old door was replaced by two half doors, beautifully carved and designed, and are in memory of King George 5th, and his Beloved wife, Queen Mary, and their Coronation as one can see by the inscription on the design, again I have the pleasure of being the one chosen to sketch the design of the doors, for the Approval, and acceptance, of the Architect in London, hanging from the rafter in the Porch, is a red glass iron frame lamp, which holds a candle for lighting the entrance to the church, but which now, is not used, the water scoop in the wall was found in the course of renovation, and is believed to have been used by the early Century worshippers, to wash their hands, (or fingers) before entering in for worship, on the opposite side of the door can be seen a small piece of stoned, or pebbled wall, this is where a piece of old wall was taken out, to see if there was a second water scoop like the first one but nothing was found, and so it was filled in again as can be seen. on the outside of the Porch, and above the door, are the Words of Our Beloved Lord, carved into woodwork. 'Come unto Me'. above thse words, there was placed in 1912, a Wooden Crucifix, depicting the Sacrifice of God's Beloved Son, Jesus Christ, upon Calvarys Cross. This was a Magnificent piece of Carving, and was supposed to be all in one piece, and was fastened to the Cross by wooden nails, but sad to say, the weather proved to all who saw it, that it was of several pieces of carving, the arms, etc, of seperate pieces, and after several years of Service, it deteriorated, and fell to the ground, never to be replaced. Now what about the life and attendance at the Church in General, well, here we have a tale to tell, lets go back to 1905. My Father, Mr S mitchell, became Verger, taking over from an older man Mr Lily who retired, and held the post until 1945, when ill health caused him to hand the position over to my Sister Elizabeth, who still holds that position, at the age of 74 years of age. My Mother, Mrs Jane Mitchell, became Caretaker of the Church, also in 1905, and also did the Alter flowers every week until she passed to higher Service in 1914, this again (the Caretaking) passed to my Sister Elizabeth, who still carries out both duties of Verger and Caretaker, and both her, and myself, who was in the Service of the church for 25 years, often have a very sad heart together, as we see our Beloved Church falling ever backward, and to decay, with apparently little interest, if any, by the Villagers as a whole. Yes, life in the Church, in the early years of the 1900, and onwards to 1916, was something that was alive, and pleasing to God. Church Services three times on Sunday, the Communion Service at nine clock, in the morning, Mattins at eleven, Communion again at twelve oclock, especially on Festival days, such as Easter, Christmas, etc, and Evensong at 3 pm in the Afternoon, Sunday School was held at 10–15 am in the old School, now a Village hall, after which at 10–45 am we marched to Church, and pleased to do so, and if, by any chance, a child missed attending, the Rector would be visiting the Parents on Monday morning, to know the reason why he, or her, was away, so we went regularly, fine weather, or wet, but not always weatherproof, today there is no poorness in family life, although one is led to believe otherwise, but, in my school-days, life was different, especially for the children, what about this for example, we very often attended school, or Sunday School, with the toes out of our shoes, and in wet weather, with wet feet too, while others perhaps could be seen wearing old shoes, far too big, being stuffed with rag wrapped round the feet to create warmth, and size. these rags had to be dried in wet weather, each time of coming home, and then used again for the next journey, to get wet again, I have myself, worn an old pair of goloshes over my worn out boots, tied on with string, to brave the inclement weather, but we enjoyed it all, and we took no harm, our

Heavenly Father took care of us. from 1905 until 1916, we had a Church Choir, consisting of up to twenty four men, and boys, and about twelve to fourteen Women, and Girls, and always in our places in Church on Sunday, I remember one Harvest Festival the Rector, announced to the choir during the Previous week, at the Practice, held friday evenings, that he had invited the Choir of Long Melford Church, to come and assist us in the singing during the Festival Services here at Alpheton, this announcement caused us some displeasure, as we considered ourselves very musical, and capable, which we were, however, several Choir men, and boys came, leaving of course, enough members of their team at Long Melford for the Services there, but on their arrival here, the Revd Bartrum found they were his only Choir, as all of us Alpheton members went on strike, and sat in the body of the Church, needless to say, this did not happen again. One amusing incident I would like to record in passing. one of our elder members of the choir, whose name must remain anonymous, had the misfortune one Sunday lunch time, in indulging rather too freely at the Red Lion inn, however, not too freely to stop him coming to the Afternoon Service, but on reaching the Church Porch, stepping down the two steps, proved a little too much for him, and he stumbled to the floor, his Wife was accompanying him, and so to cover up his distress, commented to him, 'There, I told you so, and you didn't take any notice of what I said, you've got your shoes laced up too tight,' to other peoples amusement. Choir Supper at Christmas was a great occasion, and the high light of the year, with the two Church Wardens, the four Sidesman, together with outside friends all attending, and subscribing, to make it a glad occasion, after Supper in the Rectory drawing Room, the room would be cleared, and we were entertained by the Rectors two children, Christopher, and Helen, with their Mother Mrs Bartrum at the Piano, and sometimes by the Springet brothers from Lavenham, afterwards some more refreshment, if needed, and closing with 'Auld Lang Syne', a very happy time, and enjoyed by all. In Mid Summer, until the 1914 war broke out, which needless to say took the flower of our young Men, some of whom never returned, and also which proved the first step of our Choir breaking, we had an Annual trip to the Seaside, sometimes Clacton, or perhaps Felixstowe, then Walton, quite a different trip from today, when the day arrived, we would have to start off at Six oclock in the morning, our transport to Melford Railway Station, was by means of two Millars vans (four wheeled) kindly lent by Mr W. J. Ruffle of Alpheton Mill. these vans were drawn by four farm horses, two on each van, (double shafts,) and kindly supplied, by Mr J Underhill, of Clapstile Farm, one being driven by my Brother Fred, and the other one by Mr Swallow, Mrs Eady's Father, The Union Jack was flown from each van, with seats placed all round covered by sacks or bags to sit on, on arriving at the Station, horses had to be stabled, and fed, for the day, after which we boarded the train in two reserved carriages, and then, away, reaching our destination seaside sometime before Lunch, but round about eleven, forty five, we took packed sandwiches for midday lunch, and Lemonade, (or cold tea) but at four oclock, tea was provided at a Restaurant, and kindly given by the Rector and Churchwardens, being enjoyed by all, and then the return journey about 5–30 pm arriving home, by means of the same transport round about ten oclock, and ready for bed. perhaps you may ask, times and money couldn't be all that bad, if we could find money to spend at the seaside, well, what about this, and it is the truth, my Sister Elizabeth, and I, on one occasion had the vast amount of sixpence between us to spend, our Mother being ill in bed at the time, and naturally Father did not accompany us, so we went together, and with instructions from Father who gave us the sixpence, not to spend it silly, on our arrival at the Seaside, our days spending consisted of one halfpenny currant bun, and a glass of

Lemonade costing one penny. this we shared between us, and brought fourpence halfpenny home to Father, and proud to do so. Bicycle parades were a novel feature at the Church, organised by the Rector, and attended by cyclists from near, and far, often the cycles would have some decoration, and now a few words concerning the Festivals, they were all well attended. and the church tastefully decorated by many willing helpers, Easter saw a wonderfull display of spring flowers, during Good Friday afternoon, we children would go out into the surrounding fields to gather Moss, violets, and wild primroses, these we would bunch for the Ladies, who decorated the Church windows with them, a moss foundation, with violets, primroses, and daffodils, peeping out from it, and one can imagine the fragrant perfume that was given off on Easter Sunday, to meet you at the door as you entered, from all the beautiful flowers that filled the entire church, including Arum Lilies in four large pots from Shimpling Thorne Court, young, as we children were, we felt the sacredness of our Beloved Church, and the divine presence of our Blessed Lord, as we go back in memory to these much loved times. As regards to the Annual Harvest Festival Services, what a thrill it was, to see the attendance of people from Alpheton, Bridge Street, and all the surrounding Villages, for our Harvest Festival was as a magnet of attraction. Huge crowds arrived for the Friday evening Service, while Sunday was no exception, I can still see, as I look back, the Church Packed to capacity from all denominations, even inside the Alter Rails, the chancel and main aisle full together with the Vestry, and Porch, which after the Service had to be cleared of the people to let the choir down from the stalls, not only that, the pathway from the gate to the church Porch was filled with people who could not enter the church, while many had to go home without gaining listening distance at all. The Church tastefully decorated by the Ladies of the Parish, assisted by the Rectors

Wife, Mrs Bartrum, was a sight I shall never forget. Fruit, vegetables, Corn, and flowers of every kind, together with Giant Mangolds, Swedes, Colerabbies, and eight foot towering Maize in flower, each occupying a place unto itself, crying out in adoration and Praise, to its Heavenly Creator. all this of course was before 1916, in the Revd Bartrums Incumbrancy, during which everyone in the Village had a part to play, and was happy to do it. Church-Wardens, and Sidesman were always in attendance, as they should be, setting an example to others, to follow, my brother Fred had to be early at Church to see to the ponies, and traps that brought the people to worship from the Farms, as cars were as yet unknown, and I recall on one occasion he was a little bit late, and so was hurrying along on his cycle, to be in time, going down the steep hill, his cycle brake failed to act, and he could not turn the bend at the bottom, but went clean over the hedge into the Meadow the other side, an old Gentleman, by Name, also going to Church, saw the incident, and exclaimed to my brother, who was unhurt, 'That'll larn ye ont ut,' thas where ye laid larst. yes, all festivals were kept in the Church during those years, Ash Wednesday, Good Friday, and Ascension Day, Mr Underhill, farmer of Clapstile, on Good Friday morning, called his employee's together, with this intimation, I will give you each one, who goes to Church this morning, the rest part of the day off, anyone not going, will work all day. I need not tell you what happened. And now, I turn to a different aspect, in 1916, the Revd Bartrum relinquished His Incumbrancy at Alpheton, and moved away to Billericoy, and with his Departure, the Life of the Church fell into decline, and whatever the Records of the Church show, I speak from what I know to be true. In His Place came the Revd Trousdale, a Bachelor bringing his aged Mother to live with him, as I wrote earlier on, the 1914 War, depleated our Choir Membership, but now it was to gradually die, although for a time it seemed to flourish, old

Members had gone to Serve their country, and some new Choristers were installed, but the good days were gone, the Rector seemed to be a flaw, rather than an asset. The Church structure soon began to deteriorate, and huge peices of Masonry fell from the tower. The beautiful roses in the Church yard in time broke their stake ties, and perished through neglect, those in Church office could not get along with the Rector, and after a time left to be replaced by others with little interest, and so it came about that a meeting had to be called to see what could be done in regards to the upkeep of the Church in General, one item in Particular was the tower Structure, which was now in a bad and sorry state and so as not much money was at hand to use, the Rector suggested that a six feet deep roll of wire-netting be purchased to wrap round the top of the Tower to keep masonry from falling, you may imagine the feelings of the people present, when asked to subscribe towards the cost, as one member present answered, oh yes, of course I will help, if some one present will provide the netting, I will provide the wire netting holes, amid laughter, and so on through the years with Various Rectors coming and going, at last The Revd Williamson arrived with his Wife, who endeared themselves to all, they were the first to occupy the New Rectory built between the two parishes of Alpheton, and Shimpling-Thorne, which had been amalgamated together, in the Former Rectors time, the Revd Trousdale, but which had remained apart until the Revd Lawson-Foster took charge, and who had to help him with the two parishes, a Church Army Padre, by name Capt Dauber, at this time the old Rectory was sold, but of that more later, The induction of the Revd Williamson to this parish of Alpheton, together with Shimpling Thorne, took place in 1934, in the first World War, he had served his Country as a private in the Army, being posted abroad for active Service. afterwards being ordained as a Rector, His Dear Wife designed the New Rectory, which was built for them, being equal distance from each Church. Alpheton Church however, was the dearest to his heart, He very soon after his arrival, on seeing the condition of the Church Structure, took off his coat, and set to work. helpers gathered round him, to aid him in the task of Restoration and the work was undertaken by 'Garrod Brothers' builders of Lavenham. Thousands of letters were written by the Rector to friends near, and far asking for financial help, and donations soon began to pour in, in small sums, and also fairly large, I must record first of all, that each Member of the Royal Family, (at that time) sent a gift individually towards the cost, The Present Queen Mother, Lady Elizabeth Bowes Lyon, sent a Roll of Scotch Tweed, which was sold in lengths, and realised quite a sum of Money, The Revd Bartrum, (former Rector) sent three separate Gifts of a Pound each. A Learned writer sent a book to be sold, and even the signatures of the Rectors friends near and far, were taken from letters and sold, to provide money, even so, it left much to be gathered in to realise the sum necessary for complete restoration, so six members (us of Alpheton) went round the Village collecting for the fund, and gathered in Sixty Pounds, to help, all for the Love of our dear old Church, I must record the kindness of Mr Garrod who did the work, which is, he kindly consented to receive the amount of money involved, in small or larger amounts, as it came in, but did not slack in the work until completion, the old oak wood that was taken from the tower, upon which the bells hung, much of it was used in making tea pot stands, Candle sticks, and small trays, etc, afterwards being polished, and sold to provide cash, and the final deficit was realised, by a clay pigeon shoot, organised by Mr W Wallace, of Ford Hall, Long Melford. Thus the (then Colossal) debt was paid, off, amounting between sixteen hundred, and two Thousand Pounds, but the reader may ask, what work of Restoration had to be done, let me outline it to you, as near as I can. First the Tower was unsafe, massive chunks of masonry had fallen to the ground from the top, despite the wire netting that had been wrapped round, to protect it, this left gaping holes, and provided fresh danger, by allowing the flint stones to loosen, so the whole tower from bottom to top had to be re-set, and restored, also the top ceiling of Lead was deteriorated and let the weather in, this was replaced by new Lead, and also the wooden beams of oak beneath it inside the tower the belfry structure had to be removed, and massive new beams installed, The two bells rehung, and here we pause a minute to record, that formally, the two bells could be rung quite easily, because, the bell ropes attached, led first from the base of the bell tongue, then along a short distance to a small pulley wheel, down through a belfrey floor to the Vestry beneath, thus even a young lad could ring them both quite easily, but since the rehanging of the bells, at the time of the Restoration The bell tongues were replaced by two others of a different type, these tongues have a Spring attached, upon which the bell rope is tied leaving the tongue free, the pulley wheels were removed, and the rope descends straight down through the floor, and to the Vestry beneath, and so it proved to be difficult to ring more than one bell at a time, (a pity, but it is so) much reinforcement of the belfry floor had to be done, and so on to the body of the Church, all the ouside tiling of the roof had to be replaced, and walls plastered at various places, including the buttresses as well, the interior plaster ceiling was taken down, as it was badly cracked and decaying, this revealed the beams, and stays of woodwork, which had hithertoo not been seen, these were stained and looked beautiful, the seating which was very old, consisted of closed in pews, some of which were left in position at the Rear of the church, behind the Entrance door, to leave on record the type of seating originally used, all the rest were taken out, and the present modern seating installed, these look much better, but have reduced the seating capacity. in the Chancel, I have already spoken of the two front seating stalls being removed, and replaced by much smaller, ones, to my mind this has spoilt the beauty of the Chancel, as the former ones were fully enclosed by a beautiful carved framework of Wood, with figure heads at either end, all the interior walls, which previously had been coloured Pink, were cleaned down, and coloured in a cream tint, thus providing and reflecting a lighter atmosphere, for people to see, during divine Worship, placed on the right hand wall of the body of the Church, are two Memorial Tablets in memory of the dear Lads of Alpheton, and Bridge Street, who gave their Lives in the Gallant cause of Freedom during the two World Wars, Their earthly remains lie amid the Poppies fields of France, & Belgium. during the early twenties of 1900, a second-hand Pipe Organ was purchased and erected in the Church, firstly on the Left Side of the Church where the Pulpit now Stands, afterwards being removed, and installed at the rear in the last window behind the entrance door, this was manipulated by the organist in Charge, and a hand-blower, (Mr H Long,) but after a few years Service, it was dismantled, and scrapped, owing to the dampness of the Church, not allowing it to provide adequate Music, and Tone, Visitors to the Church, and other parishioners will no doubt have noticed a Cavity behind the pulpit in the Wall, containing Steps in the fabric, but leading nowhere, this cavity, and Steps were revealed, during the Incumbrancy of the Revd H H Bartrum, who had the Masonry removed, which shewed signs of covering up something which lay behind, and it has been suggested over the Years, that these stone steps led up to a Rood Screen somewhere above, but although these suggestions still linger, nothing more than can be seen was ever found. well, these are the Loving Memories I have of this Dear old Church, to which I was taken at the tender age of a few weeks old, Memories which I shall take with me to my last resting place in the consecrated ground outside. I have only one sad thought about it all. why, oh why, has it fallen into this state of Disinterest by Officials, and parishioners alike, My Earnest prayer is that Almighty God will raise up true Followers, who will restore the Faith, and Worship in this Building that was erected so many years ago, to His Honour and Glory. We take a Walk now for exactly a Mile to Alpheton Rectory, for it is that distance from the Church Porch doors, to the front door of the Rectory, being measured by a Meter on a Cycle wheel, and here we find a building of much beauty and interest, knowing as I do, every inch of the place, I will go back to the time of my first employment there as backhouse boy. but first let us look round, [it is] a large and soundly built building surrounded by Trees, and lovely lawns, and has very fine views, in 1844, the Value of this fine old Rectory was assessed at Ten pounds, and had an adjoining meadow of some four to five acres, and six fields, of approximately 37 acres, thus totalling an acreage of about 42, a Large Storage barn, still stands as a Studio, a large fish pond, and a huge garden, also a small Stack Yard adjoining the barn, together with Coach house, two Stables to accommodate three Horses, Two for the land, and one Driving hackney, and of course the inevitable Harness Room, with a small Stove to provide warmth when occupied by the Hostler, or Coachman. Now just for a moment, let me tell you of two humorous incidents that occurred during the Incumbrancy of the Revd Aislabee, who lived here in the Rectory, but just before my time of Recolection, My Father remembered it well and told me the tale, An old Rustic lived in the Village, (I remember him well) by name. Frederick Goshawk, who would never tell his age to anyone, but always said, and declared, He went to School, until he could spell S.t.O.P, and could read P.O.J.Mouse, and then the School would have him no longer, but to my Story, This Rustic was engaged by the Revd Aislabee to clean out the pond, (being dry) and he was to throw out the mud all round the outside, so it could be carted away, and during the time he was working,

The Rector kept a watch on him, to see he didn't slack work. This irritated Fred, to such an extent that he made up his mind to put a stop to it, so, on the Rectors next trip to the edge of the pond, Fred dug his wooden mud spade into some muddy sludge, and smacked it full into the good mans face, instantly exclaiming, 'Oh Sir, I am Sorry, I didn't see you there', this of course as you will imagine, ended the Rectors vigil, on another occasion, while on his visiting rounds of the Parish, the Rector met Fred, and his first words to him, were, 'Ah Goshawk, Im going to give you a penny', to which Fred answered politely, 'Thank You Sir,' imagine his consternation at the Rectors reply, 'Ah Goshawk, you're covetous, you said Thank You before you got it, I shant give it to you now.' and he didn't. but back to the Rectory, my first memories of this place and building dates back to around 1905, or thereabout The tithe Land as it was called was rented by Mr J Underhill of Clapstile Farm, from the Incumbrant, the Revd H. H. Bartrum, while the meadow was retained for Haying purposes for the driving pony or hack as it was called. This meadow was cut Annually and stacked in the little stackyard by the Barn, carefully thatched by my Father, and kept for Winter use in the Stable, when in later years the Pony was sold, together with the coach, (Landaure), the hay was still cut and Stacked and later sold to Newmarket racing Stables, as it was such good quality hay, and fetched a good price. The Garden which is very large, was fully cultivated, and contained every consievable known flower of that time, also fruit of every kind, (except peaches), the fruit was encaged to protect it from the birds, and last but not least every kind of Vegetable. thus providing ample fresh fruit, flowers, and Vegetables all the Year round, here perhaps, I ought to record, that four Male Servants were employed outside in the spacious grounds, My Father, as head Gardiner, Mr J Simpson, as under gardiner, John Moatt a teenager for rough work, and Mr Ike Minns, Hosler, looking after the Pony, and filling in time in the garden, just outside the Garden gates (the Posts of which still stand) was a tool shed, and close by was a huge potting shed, cum, Green-house, where all flower seedings, and Brassica seedlings were raised, and hardened off for the Garden, no rose bushes were bought, although they could be seen everywhere in the grounds, in a profusion of bloom, and fragrance, all through the Summer months, these, both Standard, and bush, were raised by my Father, from cuttings yearly taken at Pruning time from the bush roses, and the standards arose, from wild briar stems from the hedgerows of Clapstile Farm, and which were budded in March and April, from special buds purchased from Cants Nurseries of Colchester, and grafted on to these wild briars, on the Left of the Cement path leading to the House was the large Croquet Lawn, where the Ladies of the District together with Mrs Bartrum would occasionally gather for a game of croquet while at the same time the Gentlemen, (Husbands of the Ladies in question) would join the Rector in a game of Tennis on the Tennis lawn, at the extreme top end of the Meadow, these occasions generally took the form of Garden parties, and after I myself in 1910 became backhouse boy, these garden parties were a big occasion for me, as some of the Visiting Ladies and Gentlemen would be driven up by their coachmen, same in Cabs, and perhaps Landaurs or something similar, their ponies or hackneys, were stabled and fed, and the Coachmen would also have tea in the kitchen. I had to be at hand to take and deliver messages to and from the house, so of course I too had my tea in the kitchen. this was a highlight to me, as delecacies for poor people was a thing unknown in those days, the higher Class lived well, but paid their Servants low wages, we ourselves as a family, Grandmother, Father, and Mother, together with Six in Family, until we started at the Eldest one earning a small wage, following on one by one, we had to live on ten Shillings a week, and afterwards eleven, as a family of nine. these were the good old days one often hear about, however, enough of that, we lived Thank God, although we could have eaten more. on the right of the Cement path, which is now a lovely lawn, and flower beds, was the Orchard, filled with Apple, pear, and Plum trees, as also some quinch bordering the Moatt which feed the pond holding hundreds, perhaps more, of fish, mostly perch, many Goldfish were put in at 1912, with the perch, by the Rector, but these have become extinct, although the Perch have flourished. in front of the Rectory is a round Lawn, with a round rose bed in the centre, when I first knew it, and until several years after, in addition to this centre bed, the Lawn also contained thirty three smaller circular beds, in which was planted a Standard Rose of about four feet high, each one being different in Name, Colour, and fragrance, can you picture it dear Reader, on a Summers day morning, to smell the fragrant Perfume that arose to your nostrels, as you stood and gazed upon that magnificent splendour of God-given beauty, it is something that I shall never forget, a something that draws me very, very close indeed to a Blessed and Loving Saviour. on the Left of the House is a side Lawn which had existed as long as I can remember, also a little copse or Spinney, which I knew as the Wilderness, and contained in my early years, a little Summer house, where one could sit and read, if so preferred, while being alone, and partly screened from all else, or perhaps to cool off from the heat of the day. beside this stood a little maple tree, or Stub if you like to call it such, and this was covered from all sides by Mistletoe. This has long since become extinct, as also the Summer house. let us take a look round to the back of the Rectory, quite a different outlook now to what it used to be, for in my early recollections servants were kept severely apart from their employers, so instead of a clear view from the kitchen window, there was a six foot high trellis work running from between the Study window and kitchen window out to the drive, this was engulfed by massive Laurels, to shut out any view from the grounds outside, immediately in front of the kitchen was a small sewage well, with a small pump affixed, this well of course took all household water etc, and had to be pumped out by hand from time to time and disposed of among the laurel shrubs round about, The Back yard was shut off too by a tall wooden fence (still existing), on one side, and a brick wall with an entrance tradesmans gate on the other, and woe betide anyone going to the front door by mistake. The Barn, or studio as it is now called, in the years when the land was farmed by the Incumbrant, was the Storing place for the Corn, it had large entrance doors, where the small door and window now are, one can have proof of this, by observing the old fashioned heavy iron hinge, (or staple) still there, but when Mr J Underhill hired the land from the Revd Bartrum, when he came as Rector, the Barn just remained idle, apart from odd uses, it was converted into a Studio, by a Mr Reynolds, a later owner of the Rectory, during the second World War for the purpose of concerts, and films being held, to help to keep the people of the Village cheerful, and as happy as possible, while their young Sons, and fiancees, were enveloped in the great struggle for liberty, and freedom, one more recollection before we enter the Rectory house. the lovely drive in those days was a tarred drive from top to bottom, (now gravelled, and stoned) again we see great massive Laurels on either side at intervals, and were clipped yearly, and shaped into large squares, anyone could hide themselses in these great Shrubs, and not be seen. At the Bottom of the Drive, a Large iron decorated Gate hung on two wooden Posts, painted white, and had by the order of the Rector to be closed every night, and opened again in the morning, this was to ensure safety from straying cattle, or horses, very prevalent in those days, straying Gipsy horses in particular, and aslo to ensure privacy as well, the iron gate that hangs there now at the present time, was at that time hung at the Top end of the drive, just above the fork where one road leads off to the barn, and gardens. this also was painted white, as also the two posts, again wooden ones, we will pause here for a moment, to relate an amusing incident which happened to my father, and I one very dark Winter evening, I had been waiting for the letters to Post on my way home, this I might add was one of my duties as back-house boy, for although my day finished at five P.M. I had to wait in the kitchen sometimes until five fifty five, for letters to post for the evenings collection, which went out at Six oclock, these letters, and postcards, would be numerous, any number up to twenty sometimes to be stamped and posted, and if by chance there was any change out of the money given me for stamps, this had to be taken back, before going home, so the reader will see I was taught to work the hard way to earn my living, from 6 oclock until often six oclock, six days a week, for the wonderful wage of five shillings per week. my pocket money? one penny. however, to my amusing incident, as it was such a dark night, my father waited for me, and we had been talking, (the Servants) about Ghosts, so, on recieving the letters, we started off side by side from the Rectory, after a few minutes walk, my father suddenly stopped, and without a word gripped my hand in a firm clasp, and there, standing beside us was a tll ghostly figure, clad in white from top to toe, hardly daring to breathe, we stood motionless, waiting for the apparition to make the first move, but it didn't, and then, with a laugh, father said to me, 'Come on', realising what appeared at first to be a ghost, was in reality the white painted gate post at the top of the drive, with the gate standing open at the opposite side, shutting the gate firmly, we hurried off with the letters to post. So much for the outside, so now we will go indoors, and we find a large roomy, and spacious interior, containing a large entrance Hall, Dining Room, (very much modernised to its earlier condition, spacious Drawing Room, where the Annual Choir Supper always took place, crossing over a long passage way, we find a nice cosy room, which was earlier the nursery and school room for the Rectors Children, next the Apple cupboard, followed on by the Butlers Pantry, kitchen, Servants Pantry, Larder, and Cooks Cupboard, Sculury, Back-door entrance Hall, and further on, the Game larders, also indoor Cellar, used for raising, Chicory, Salsify, and indoor seakale, very popular in those days for Salads, just outside the back door was the large Coal Cellar, which very often contained a depth of water, much to the Cooks annoyance, the little pump that was used to draw out this water, can still be seen fitted to the wall outside, in the scullery still stands the large pump fitted to a very deep well, which supplied water to all parts of the house, both upstairs and down, this water had to be pumped by hand night and morning into large galvanised tanks situated at various parts of the building, pipes led too and from these tanks, giving water to hand wherever needed. there was never any need for P.T, after filling up, I was usually ready for my breakfast. in the large scullery, were two very large Coppers, but I only remember one being in use, this was used for the Clothes-wash weekly, and fed of course by a Coal or wood fire. the farther game Larder was converted into toilets during the 1939–45 War, of which more later, in the kitchen can be seen high up in the Wall, a small window, which opens into the Butlers Pantry, this was used in former days, to pass Crockery, or Cutlery etc from the Kitchen to the Butler, for the Butlers pantry was his domain, and so, '*Dont you dare to come in here*', hence the little window. also fitted to the kitchen wall were two glass and wooden frames, in which could be seen, a small square slot, one for each room of the front of the house, and for all rooms upstairs, a set of bells, (old fashioned) were fitted on the Wall in the passage just outside the Drawing room, these were all operated by a switch, one in each room, and fed by the old fashioned acid in water, on pressing one of these buttons, or switches, a little card would drop into one of the little slots in the Kitchen, this would tell the Parlour Maid to which Room she had to go. Perhaps I ought to say here, that beside the outdoor employees, the indoor Servants comprised,—Cook, Butler, House-parlour-maid, and Backhouse-boy, being myself, this was of course, all in the Revd Bartrums time, until 1916, when he went away, which as you will understand, altered all of which I am telling you now. from downstairs to upstairs, and here we find a room with bow windows, this was the Rectors Study, where all his Sermons were compiled, and of course, gave him a very fine view of all activity outside, for no one was allowed to dither, adjoining this was the boot Room, a tiny room over the front door, next is a Room that was used for the children as a bedroom, (unless of course the Baby years of Life were outlived, this also was occupied by their nursery governess, (if any), a few more steps, and here we find two steps up to a large Room, namely the Visitors Room, with two windows overlooking the french Window of the Drawing Room below, crossing over the intervening Passage, is another room to be seen, again containing two windows overlooking the Wilderness, this was known as [?] and occupied by the Rector and his Wife, a little further on, and another Room, overlooking the back door, again a Visitors Room, if not otherwise engaged. now we turn to the Right, and here is the first Butlers Room over the Butlers Pantry, and next door, another room, not very often used but still furnished and available as a Bedroom. above all this, are the Attic-rooms, high up in the Roof, here were the Cooks and Parlour-maids apartments reached by back stairs from the Kitchen, and overlooked the backyard, outside the bedroom window was suspended an old-fashioned spring bell, with a long chain attached, and which led down to the ground this bell had to be rung each morning at six-oclock to wake up the maids, either by the Gardiner, or back-house boy. Yes, hours had to be strictly kept, with Breakfast at eight oclock sharp, for the Cook, her work, was in the kitchen, for the parlourmaid, downstairs rooms to tidy, three perhaps fôur fires to light, table for breakfast to set etc, for the backhouse boy, water to pump up, sticks and coal to fetch, not to mention anything up to nine pairs of boots, and Buskins to clean, and walking shoes for the Ladies, I remember, one morning, I had extra cleaning to do, and the water pumping had taken extra time, so I hurried over the boots to catch up. this led to the cleaning of them not proving Satisfactory to the Rector, so, as I had gone to breakfast, he placed them all outside the back door in a row for me to clean again on my return, but, during the breakfast hour, it had rained for a while, and no one having noticed it, matters were made worse by all the boots being wet inside, needless to say, this didn't happen again. well now, you think, have Eddie forgotten anything, as I have not mentioned the Bathroom, oh dear me no, no bathroom, for a bath was unheard of in those days, a good wash oh yes, but a bath, that was asking for pneumonia, to say the least about it. Well, before we leave this fine old Rectory for elsewhere in the Village, I must record, that like many another, it had the reputation for being haunted, for up to as far as 1944, noises were heard, and ghostly figures were reputed to be seen, but strangely enough, everything was confined to the Visitors bedroom, where two steps led up to it, indeed no servant would ever leave the room except by walking backwoods, so as to be able to catch hold of the door, as it would inevitably slam shut upon them otherwise, strange noises of heavy footsteps walking about the room could be heard, while the room bell would constantly ring at night for hours on end, calling in the register in the kitchen for attendance in this particular room, needless to say no one, or anything could be found, on one occasion, my father was asked to sleep in the house alone, as the entire household were away on holiday, including the Servants, so after having supper at home, he went back to the Rectory, and after satisfying himself all was in order, he went to bed and to sleep, but not for long, for after a while, he woke up feeling cold, and to find the bedclothes which covered him all gone, so, getting up from the bed, he discovered them on the floor beside, so thinking perhaps he had tossed, and turned, he proceeded to replace them, and did so, but as he was about to return to bed again, they all disappeared over the other side as before, this was repeated again, so my father decided he was an unwanted guest, and come down-stairs for the rest of the night, but all the Years that the Mitchell Family have been connected with the Former Rectory, nothing was ever seen in Person, although on one occasion it was stated by a Teenage Land Girl, that a ghostly figure similar to an old Lady clad in a shawl, stood watching her at the foot of the bed, How did the Rectory become an Ex-Rectory? let me tell you, on the Retirement or should I say resignation of the Revd Trousdale, the Place stood empty for a while, and became derelict and overgrown, the Church Services being conducted by the Revd Lawson Foster (living at Melford) and helped by an Elderly Church Army Captain, who had come to reside in Alpheton at Fir Tree Cottage, his name? Captain Dauber, who eventually married the Widow of Mr Fred Bowd, and they were for some time an asset to the Villages of Alpheton, and Shimpling, which became Amalgamated together about this time, However the Revd Foster declined to live in Alpheton Rectory, and so it was sold by Auction, and bought by a Mr F Ince of Shimpling a builder by trade, having purchased, he did the place up somewhat, and again put it up for sale. Two people were greatly interested, and each were willing to pay the required price, so, Mr Ince made a stipulation that whichever Client was willing to pay him an Extra Ten Pounds for it would be the Owner, and so it became the property of Mr Owen Reynolds, He, and His Wife, and Baby Daughter, together with His Mother-in Law, a Mrs Tyler, were in residence from 1935 until 194 . engaging two Servants, and one Nursery Governess, but from that time and onwards, no one else was ever employed in the grounds outside, what little work was done, was carried out by each owner, I have already mentioned the conversion of the Barn into a Studio, and for what purpose, by Mr Reynolds, so we will pass over to the time of His joining the Government Forses, going into the Army as an Interpreter, but very soon afterwards being invalided out through illness, eventually passing away with Cancer in the Throat, and was buried in Alpheton new Burial ground. The Rectory now passed into the possession of Commander Hutchinson, a Submarine Commander, but he, being in the Services did not take possession until the conclusion of World War 2, so, it was occupied for a time by the Womens Land Army, who later joined the Land Army Branch at Shimpling park Farm, Several of these Girls found partners in the surrounding vicinity, and are now the proud Wives of their Loving Husbands, who became attracted to them in the first place, by their different acent of Speech, for instance, Yorkshire, Halifax, etc, On their departure from the Rectory, it became a prisoner of War Camp for a time, housing thirty Italians, very sociable young men, and well behaved, although their mode of cooking was somewhat different to ours in England, for example, all their meat would be cooked on top of the kitchen range, but in no utensils, so imagine where the grease, or dripping ran to. When war finished, these fine chaps returned home to Italy and the owner of the Rectory (Commander Hutchinson) returned, and stayed with his young Wife and baby, until 1947, being succeeded by General Freeland, He, and his Wife, one Daughter, and two Sons, his sons being in the Services and away most of the time, these people moved away in 1957 and took up Residence at Brent Eleigh Hall, after them came Colonel Haimsworth and his Wife, their two grown up Children living abroad, Mrs Haimsworth was a big asset to the Church, while living here, these people moved away to Cavendish in 1966, being Succeeded the same year by its Present owners Mr & Mrs Morriss, long may they stay with us, Mr Morriss is at Present, Peoples Warden in the Church.

Now we must start our journey through the Village, this will take us a long time, as we have several stops, and much to record, so we will cross the fields to the corner of the Village and our first stop will be:—

'Clapstile Farm,'

Formerly Clap Farm, and Formerly, Andrewes Farm, This holds many happy, and sad Memories for me, as I have seen so many—many changes during the years of my employment there, some of which I will write. Clapstile always spell home to me, as the Mitchells Family have had connection with it well over one hundred and Fifty Years, First my Great Uncle Robert Turner, secondly my Dear Mother, who married my Father from there, next my Brother Fred, also my Brother Bert, also my Sister Elizabeth, who was domestic in the house, and Land Girl during World War I, and Lastly myself, being stockman to four generations, I would like, when my time come, to be buried on one of its fields, but realise of course, the impossibility of this, but the Memories of it through the Years I shall take with me, I record first of all that it was farmed by a Mr Bear, who still has a relative living in Acton, and it was to this Man that my Mother was servant, times were bad, and my Mother had a very small wage but happy in her employment, having left the Angel Hotel at Bury St Eds to come there. Mr Bear was succeeded by Mr J Underhill, who came in 1897 from Devonshire, and who pulled the farm together to make it a good and sound investment, He stayed 24 years, and retired on £4,000 Pounds Capital, but what of the Farm and buildings, my recollections are of a large farm house, containing Lounge, Dining Room, and kitchen, with a long Hall dividing kitchen from the rest of the rooms downstairs, the kitchen, and scullery adjoining, together with a Pantry, as you may already realise by the long passage was the Servants quarters, but of course as only my sister was domestic for Mrs Underhill, these servants quarters were not recognised, in the scullery was a large copper used for all purposes, clothes, dairy, etc, on the left of the kitchen door was the beer House providing home brewed bear for the employees, afterwards being turned into the dairy, 3 large bedrooms upstairs, and the room above the kitchen now a bathroom, was the so called lumber room, where Binder canvaces, and small tools, wagon ropes etc were all stored, and if any room at all to spare, Apples as well, a lovely staircase was renovated in the early 1900s, under an outside verandah is a large coal shed, built of course in the house, but approached to outside, at the far end of the verandah, is, or was a large downstairs room with a large brewing Copper, beer being brewed twice a Year, by an employee, Mr C Leeks, also in this room is a large stone slab, why is it there? Yes you have guessed it, its the pig killing slab, where a pig occasionally was killed for the house, and the large Staple, or hook in the ceiling was to hang the pig on for dressing purposes, afterwards being preserved with Salt Petre, until required, no fridges in those days, above this are two rooms one fairly large, and one small, again used in the early years as farm lumber rooms, and new farm tools, such as spades, forks, draining tools etc, these rooms later became farm offices. formerly farm tools had to be provided by the employee. When I was employed by Mr Underhill, for the satisfactory wage of Six shillings per week, the hours being from Seven in the morning until five oclock at night, for Six days per week as there were no holidays apart from Christmas Day at that time, I well remember, when engaging me he asked, if I possessed a Spring tined, (or muck) fork, on my saying no, he promised to buy me one, which he did, but my delight at having one, was somewhat dampened when pay day came, and he took five shillings and sixpence out of my wages to pay for the fork, and I received the odd sixpence to live on until next week, the outside farm buildings are somewhat different to the former buildings of which I now write. they consisted of a large Corn barn, a five partitioned Cart lodge and several small fattening sheds, together with Cow shed for five Cows, a fairly large Cart horse Stable, to accomodate nine working horses, two riding Stables, which held a small pony for the Mistress's use, and a light hack for the Masters use, these two were commandeered by the Army in the first world war of 1914–1918, and so the only means of transport for the Master and Mistress, was an old Motor byke and side Car, this ancient machine was purchased by Mr H Ruffle in 1921, when He took over the farm from Mr Underhill who retired from farming, but to continue there were also Calf houses, and a row of piggeries, and a Meal house for mixing, also a dutch type piggery, (fattening unit) to house Sixty baconers, all these sheds for [formed?] a Circle and enclosed a large yard for the horses, one for Cows, and the remaining one for fattening red Poll Cattle, no finer cattle was produced anywhere around the district. Clapstile Farm held the esteem for good beef for many years, now my story takes on a very sad note, as a disastrous fire broke out one evening in 1958, at eight oclock in the evening, and spread with such rapidity that much damage was caused before it was controlled, The barn and all the sheds were destroyed, although many willing hands did what they could to help. and I must record here the bravery of Mrs Rix who was in bed with a cold at the time, and was alone apart from Trevor, (the Son), Mr Rix being at work at Bridge St, and myself at Shimpling She and my Sister, rushed out to the enclosed yards, and released all the animals, and drove them out through blazing straw to safety, as also a quantity of fowls, but sad to say, five Calves perished in the flames, having first been suffocated by smoke, and was close to the seat of the fire where it started, it will never be really known the cause of the outbreak, but it was assumed a spark escaped from a small generating plant. the existing buildings of Concrete soon came into being, and animal breeding, and welfare continued as before, but the reader can well imagine, that tragic evening remained in our hearts and thoughts for a long, long time, one that I, like Mr and Mrs Rix will never forget. Many changes have taken place on this farm over the years of my remembrance joyous ones, and also sad ones, but to me, it will always be home, with the kind permission of these two dear people, Mr & Mrs Rix, I am allowed to go up anytime I choose, and nothing pleases me better than to wander around the farm in my years of retirement. which bring back the memories of my working days there. and now, we must resume our journey, and we take our walk down the lovely lime tree Avenue of this farm, pausing at the Bottom for a while, and here we find a Cluster of homes, close together, which have greatly changed in Character, and design over the years of my recollection, but first of all we take a look at the pair of Cottages standing immediately in Clapstile drive, and now the property of Mr and Mrs Rix, formerly belonging to Mr Underhill, and before that they were the property of Miss Gardiner, who lived at that time, where the Alpheton Cafe stands now, these two Cottages were first of thatched roofs, and plaster walls, covered with a lime wash. their construction were long, but very low in height, the bedrooms being in the lean-to roofs, my earliest recollection is that a Mr & Mrs Welham lived in the one facing Clapstile, and a Mr & Mrs Amos, and their Son Stanley lived in the one facing the Road. it is of this family that I have much to record. No one ever knew from where they originated, but let it suffice to say they arrived somewhere around 1906. The Wife was an invalide and remained so until the time of her death, the boy

Stanley was ten years old when they came. the man himself was a real Character, setting up a shop in the room facing the road, and please remember, this was the only room downstairs apart from a small pantry, all kinds of vegetables were offered for sale, besides fruit of almost every description, these of course had to mingle with the household furniture (what there was of it), and also Crocery, and Cutlery, soon after opening his shop, he also started to cook, and sell pastry as well, seldom ever having a wash, the reader can imagine that his pastry was far from being white, however his one speciality was jam tarts, two for a penny, and this earned him the name of Tarty Amos, of course, he must have transport to get around with, and so, he bought a tate sugar box, to which he fixed a pair of iron wheels from off an iron sheep hurdle, two peices of wood for the two handles, and his transport was complete, he himself was the pony in the Shafts, now, I am pausing here for a moment to tell you something of our roads and their construction prior to 1911, they were only rough cart tracks and somewhat narrow, kept up by stones picked off the fields of Alpheton at four and six a heaping tumble load, picked up by Mothers and Children, and also by Stones (flint) from Acton Pit, followed later by rough granite, this was hardly ever rolled in, being left for the traffic of that time to roll it in themselves, our present lovely main road that we have were constructed from 1911 and onwards through the years being made eighteen feet wide instead of about twelve feet formerly, I have stated this, concerning the roads, as I want you to visualise our Mr Tarty and his transport on a road of this construction, wearing no shoes, or socks, he would pull or push, this trolley to Cockfield Station, and Collect a consignment of vegetables, potatoes, bananas, and soft fruit, where they came from, was his business, and come back fully loaded to sell in his Shop. on one occasion he was pushing his trolly home and had reached the old School, when one wheel caught against an outside stone, jerking the handles from his grasp, and spilling most of the contents on to the road, many willing Childrens hands helped to pick up the goods, but ran away with them to eat themselves. At the commencement of the year 1908, Mrs Amos deteriorated in health, and soon afterwards died, and stanley was left to the tender Mercies of his father, which were far from being that, On learning of her death, my father (being the gravedigger) naturally interviewed Mr Amos in regards to the funeral but met with little success, as also the Revd Bartrum, Rector at that time, she was to have a parish Coffin, and funeral, as no insurances were paid for that occasion, all necessities were carried out by the husband, who informed the Rector later, that the deceased lady had been removed to Lavenham for space convenience, this information was not however accepted, and so my father went up to the Cottage again, this time only the lad was at home, and so in answer to my fathers knocking at the door, Stanley answered it, and with these words he said, You've come to see Mother Mr Mitchell? I'll shew you where she is, and to my fathers astonishment, Stanley led him to an outside shed, opened the door, and exclaimed, 'There she is, as fresh as ever', and there she was, in an upright position, in the Coffin standing on end upon the dirt floor, on the funeral day, Stanley was left after the Service, to help my father fill in the grave, for said his father, it is the last thing we can do for her. later towards the end of the year in question, with the dark nights settled in and sharp frost as well, a small wisp of smoke was seen to be hovering over the thatch of the house, one afternoon, and it soon became apparent that something was wrong, evidently a fire was starting somewhere, but where? neither father or Son were at home, at the time, and as the Village people began to arrive, it became evident that a quantity of so called furniture had been removed from the Cottage and locked up in an old shed in the back garden, friends lent willing hands to remove the next door neighbours furniture and Clothing to safety, and soon afterwards the

Long Melford fire engine arrived on the scene, an old fashioned hand pumping system, requiring twelve persons on each side to work the pump, naturally the first job of the Brigade Captain (one of the four firemen) was to secure the aid of twenty four pump assistants, this took quite a while, but eventually all was ready to start, at this point Mr Amos and Son arrived home, but of course too early for their expectations, as the fire wherever it was had not shewn itself. no effort was made to assist the fireman in their duties by Mr Amos, so windows were smashed in to gain entrance, and the never fading joke to this very day by those who were there is, that the fireman lit stormlamps and searched the house upstairs and down, to find the fire, as by this time it was quite dark, after a little while of searching, a peice of plaster was found to have been removed in the lean-to roof upstairs, and an oily rag had been placed in the thatch inside and lit by a match, and the peice of plaster replaced to hide it, but lack of air kept it smouldering, until the plaster was removed as I have said, then, receiving air, away it went gutting the entire roof of the two Cottages, as the ancient fire engine, could not effectually cope with it. thus ended Tarty's stay in Alpheton, leaving as quietly, as he came, and vanished, it was afterwards Village knowledge, that he had wilfully fired the Cottage to get an insurance policy, which he had taken out against fire the previous week. opposite on the other side of the drive, where until recently there was a large peice of waste ground covered by dense undergrowth, and now taken into the field by Sir Richard Parker, stood a double tenement Cottage, made of Clay Brick walls and straw intermingled, and with a thatched roof, this double tenement was very large, with a large garden at either end, my only remembrance of this, as it was derelict and tumbling to decay, in my boyhood days, is, that I played up and downstairs in the ruins, with the other boys and girls of the Village. our great delight was to see a roof rafter fall to the ground, or a bunch of thatch, needless to say the woden rafter didn't stay long on the ground. now just round the corner of the drive, and on to the then main road stands a three tenement large Cottage, occupied by Mrs Cambell [Campbell], and Friend, who are also owners of the same, but first of all, may I recap for a moment back to the burnt out Cottage already mentioned, as I forgot to record, that the ruins were bought by Mr Underhill of Clapstile Farm, as Miss Gardiner died, and he had the whole structure restored, and then added the two kitchens and two boxrooms, one of which is now an upstairs bathroom, thus rose again the Cottages [one double dwelling] as they are seen today, and have become part of Clapstile Farm, [At time of recording 'Oiky', Len Mills and his wife, Cynthia, and his daughter, Judith, occupied the half facing Clapstile Farm] now back to Mrs Campbells Cottage, formerly known as 'Corner Houses, this too was purchased from Miss Gardiner by Mr Underhill and used by him for employees. but prior to this, the smaller cottage in the block, next to the other pair, was rented by an old couple, Man and Wife, Mr & Mrs George Mitchell, a slight, but distant relation of mine, the old man was nicknamed (fashion) as he had some old fashioned ways, this poor old couple, (and I mean poor,) for in their day, poor relief as it was called was nothing short of Starvation, consisted of 2/6 per person per week, and one loaf of Bread per two persons, if you were able to walk down to Bridge Street Rose and Crown to fetch the said loaf, you ask why Bridge Street? because that was the distribution Centre, if the persons in question were unable to go, well then, *no bread.* I remember that my mother, if she found out anyone in particular who couldn't go it for themselves, she would walk down herself and get it for them, if of course the relief officer would allow her to obtain it, for this walk, there and back, she was paid one halfpenny. also at one time, these two poor old people got behind in paying their rent to Miss Gardiner, the said rent being one shilling per week, this continued for six weeks, amounting to six shillings Now this *good Lady* in question, had pity for no one, and so, she made it her business one day to go for the rent, and on finding out they could not pay in full exclaimed, well, you cant pay, so I shall take your six kitchen chairs that you have in place of the six shillings, which she did, and straitway gave them to the Church, as a gift from herself, and they are there to this day, may God have forgiven her. some time later on, the old Lady went for a pail of water at the adjoining small pond, and coming back with it, just reached her gate and fell dead into the yard, later on, the old man was taken ill and died also, and both had parish funerals, as no money was available, perhaps here, for the benefit of present generation, and present Life, I ought to explain that a parish funeral, mean, that the deceased person of that time who had no means of providing the wherewithal for their eventual interment, this event would be taken over by the poor Law institution, who would provide a rather rough made coffin, with no varnish or furnishings of any kind, just a little square peice of wood for a breastplate, and their initials put on it, (perhaps burnt in) that was all, a rough grave maybe, and scant respect, afterwards, if the said, deceast lived alone, the house furnishings, however few, would be cleared, and sold, the moeny given of course, to the Relief institution. May such times never come back again, at one time this little Cottage was turned into a Meeting house, for Sunday Worship, A Saintly man of God living in Alpheton, in the old ruins of the Cottage known as 'Baileys', or Rose Cottage, A Working man six days a week, but on Sunday, he would be found in his beloved Meeting house at ten forty five a.m, for an hours Service in the afternoon he would be preparing for the evening Service at six thirty p.m. several people including children would attend the evening Service, and a few occasionally in the mornings, but the Services were held and the old fashioned Gospel proclaimed, congregation, or not, he would use the Sankey Solos hymn book, and his organ was one of the first Phonographs to be made, an Eddison Bell Production with a long brass Horn, two little oil lamps were used for lighting, and a coal fire for heating. He met with much opposition from the Church Rector, but he carried on faithfully in the work of the Lord for several years before his death, during the latter years of this work, he, having moved to Lawshall to live, would walk from there each Sunday, rain, or shine, winter and Summer alike, bringing his dinner, and tea with him, mostly bread and cheese tied up in a red handkerchief. oh that we had more like him today, really on their toes for Christ, and the people, not counting the cost, but following their Masters footsteps, in seeking the lost Souls for His sheep-fold, on one occasion, (and I record this, as I have been asked to put into this book, any little humorous peices) an old man (a Mister Sutton) living in the Parish, attended one Sunday evening, the Phonograph was about to play a hymn, and Mr Moss looking at the aged man, asked him, 'can you hear Mr Sutton', to which he replied, 'Yaas, Yaas, I cin hare it' but the Phonograph hadn't yet started to play. the other part of this block of Cottages was occupied by a Mr & Mrs Leeks and family, the daughter, Bertha, being employed as domestic, by Miss Gardiner, altogether there were five in family, the youngest daughter Elsie, at the tea table one evening was asked to make the tea, fetching the kettle from the fire, she was about to pour the boiling water on to the tea leaves, but before doing so, he [she] said something to her father to which she received no reply, (as was his custom) so to make him answer her, she poured a little boiling water from the kettle onto his bald head, quickly getting her reply, but not what she expected, afterwards poor old Charlie said, 'I went about with a hulk of lard on me hid for days', and no wonder for it was nicely blistered, next it was occupied by my Brother Bert who married, and after him, & his Wife came the Ponder family, it was now the property of Mr

Underhill, Miss Gardiner having died, he, it was who sank a well not far from the house for the benefit of his Tenents, the water question in the Village being almost at a crisis, especially in the Summer. After his death, this block of Cottages were bought by a Mr & Mrs Astbury, who was a Seafaring man, living there for some years, and he passed on in 1945, and his dear Wife in 1949, both are buried in Alpheton new burial ground. they were succeeded by Mr & Mrs Pitman, they too resided there for some years, Mr Pitman being a very active Member of the Village hall, (the old School) in its Early Stages, he, it was who built the existing stage for the Hall, doing the work himself, he was an asset to the Village in many ways, before he passed on, soon followed by his Wife, and they too are buried in Alpheton new burial ground. And now, the Cottages, bearing the Name of 'Talledge', have become the property of Mrs Campbell, and Mrs Gibby, long may they stay with us.
Strolling towards Bridge Street for a few moments, just before we reach the crest of Cole-Hill, on our left, we remember a small meadow and a little spinney, now all cleared away, and become part of a field, but in the meadow, stood some Cartsheads belonging to Mr W. J. Ruffle